Nantucket Atheneum Writer's Group

Copyright © 2014 Nantucket Atheneum
Cover illustration: National Oceanic and Atmospheric Administration illustration of Nantucket harbor and town. Circa 1839

All rights reserved.

ISBN: **1499613008**
ISBN-13:**978-1499613001**

# NANTUCKET

Nantucket! Take out your map and look at it. See what a real corner of the world it occupies; how it stands there, away off shore, more lonely than the Eddystone lighthouse. Look at it-a mere hillock, and elbow of sand; all beach, without a background.

Herman Melville, *Moby-Dick; Or, The Whale*

# CONTENTS

|    | Acknowledgments              | i   |
|----|------------------------------|-----|
| 1  | Sounds of the Point          | 3   |
| 2  | Island of Many Lands         | 9   |
| 3  | Ghosts of 'Sconset           | 16  |
| 4  | Coming of Age                | 21  |
| 5  | The Summer People            | 44  |
| 6  | Off Season                   | 47  |
| 7  | To Be A Beggar               | 62  |
| 8  | Coffee                       | 69  |
| 9  | From Nantucket To Mars       | 72  |
| 10 | Big Girl                     | 85  |
| 11 | Unchained                    | 91  |
| 12 | Sunday                       | 110 |
| 13 | All The Way Out to 'Sconset  | 112 |
| 14 | Run                          | 117 |

# ACKNOWLEDGMENTS

I would like to thank the members of The Nantucket Atheneum Writer's Group: The Moving Pen who show up twice a month game for whatever writing assignments I throw at them. We have written memoir, fiction, poetry, letters and journalism. We have used visual prompts, olfactory prompts (good smells only), word magnets, newspaper clippings and characters from history.

And, even though we all start from the same prompt, when each person shares their writing we go on such a dazzling variety of journeys, as close as the front door and as far away as Mars, that it's as if we have received different assignments.

A very special thank you to Kathy Butterworth and Kristine Glazer for their careful editing and reading of the book, and, for making us look good.

I am inspired by the group's creativity, support and willingness to let loose their imaginations. Writing is hard work but you make it fun.

Bravo to you all!

Amy Jenness

# 1. SOUNDS OF THE POINT

**By Julianne Kever**

Growing up on Brant Point, the fog horn was as natural a sound to me as my mother's voice yelling at one or the other of us many kids, to try and maintain order in the chaos. That horn out in the heavy veil of low moisture over dark water, was doing its best to provide safe passage to any boats needing to be out in the fog and that thought gave me comfort.

If we were outside playing the neighborhood version of hide-and-seek and the fog descended on us, we would always hear the horn before the mothers calling us back in, when they looked up from the dinner casserole or ironing board, realizing it was getting too damp to stay outside.

Its deep, eerie call was haunting as well, because I knew the fog threw sounds, played tricks with location and I could worry that someone might be lost on the other side of the channel. Sometimes I'd wonder if it was really a help after all, but knew it must be; and the Coast Guard was right there at the end of Easton Street listening and ready to help.

There was always the sound of noisy children, mainly from our own house, there being between four to ten of us, depending on if it was 1953 or 1962 at the time. A couple of kids lived behind us, two or three next to us and anywhere between three and six across the street (also depending on the year!) as our year-round neighbors. As is usual with children, we had our favorites we were eager to play with when our mother freed us from homework or housework, which seemed unending. And we had the ones we fought with or just simply didn't like, but there were enough of us to spread out the loyalties and make for some fun. The boys, of course seemed more foolish and challenging to us girls, often finding spiders or snakes to scare us away from their secret camps, if we didn't take no for an answer when we asked to join.

Someone always managed to fall off a bike or out of a tree and our mother being a nurse, took it all in stride. There was noise at every side of the house and yard, and if it was suddenly silent, you had to wonder what the pairings were up to. Maybe one was trying to find a way into our dad's 'office' in the garage, or torturing some poor bug, or whispering tales of being grown-up girls to each other. Once in a while someone got pulled from the fray, due to misbehavior that the rest of us were just lucky enough not to get caught at. If you were playing outside in those days, you were carefree, able to run and make noise, as long as you stayed within the few yards around our houses. Of course, being one of the older girls, I'd usually find myself watching a younger brother or sister and not able to run off with the rest of them, but I could hear the fun and fighting and make out which kids were at the heart of it.

As we grew older, we became more aware of others coming and going down on the Point, and they brought their own sounds along. There was the sweet black maid who worked at the Breakers for the tourist season, heading to or from work, humming to herself, minding her own business, sometimes sending out a quick smile if we were being nice children on the porch. Whatever possessed us to take our parents' 45 of Don't Be Cruel and turn it up as loud as possible when she was passing quietly by, just to watch her jump at the sudden shock of noise, I don't know! But we did it and nearly died laughing, cowards inside the house, until we realized she was an adult and could turn us in to our mom and then there'd be a different sound going on that none of us would like. As far as we could tell, she never did squeal on us, but we didn't get any more shy smiles either, when she walked by.

July Fourth meant the seasonal families and tourists had arrived and most of them were finding their way down to Jetties for the evening fireworks, so we would watch them go by on Easton Street with their picnics in hand. It felt a little funny having them take over the Point that night, while we had to stay put on the porch or watching out a second floor window of a bedroom. Our mother thought the youngest kids might actually go to sleep, until she had it proved over and again, that it wasn't going to happen with all the excitement going on and then with the relentless deep-down booms that sounded before each display bloomed in the sky. Those old fireworks had a resonating boom that you felt hit you smack in your chest. I can't remember which sibling it was, but boy did they howl with each one that went up... in sheer terror, not delight like the rest of us! The boys would act like they'd been shot, I think maybe to hide the fact that it had scared them too.

Another Summer sound we just loved, was the bell of the ice cream truck making its rounds up and down Easton, Harbor Way and Walsh, before finally getting to Willard Street where we were sure the driver must have run out of ice cream bars. We were only allowed to buy anything about once a week, our parents "not being made of money", as Dad liked to put it, so we came up with a brilliant idea one year, to give the driver a bunch of our mother's hydrangeas in exchange for ice cream bars. This he would only do in exchange for 'squishies' which were squashed rejects he couldn't sell anyway. After about two weeks of that, he figured out there were too many of us to satisfy, and he didn't need any more flowers. Actually, our mother's hydrangea bush was beginning to look like a bomb had hit it!

We could hear the summer people's dogs barking all around the Point, the knife-sharpener's bell that brought out sewing shears and kitchen knives, the barbecue parties going on and lots more cars than usual from July 4 until Labor Day, the last celebration before the summer homes were deserted and the families headed back to the mainland. Then, we once again owned the neighborhood. That's when we got back to racing through empty yards and our marathon hide-and-seek games, until the lessening evening light forced us back inside, for one television show before bed. The few year-round families who really did live there got back to school and business as usual, while a unique quiet descended on the yards, children inside with homework, and cocoa to chase away the chill.

During all the seasons though, there was one constant sound that was my favorite; it overshadowed any noise we kids could come up with and was more regular than the fog horn. It was the deep sonorous blast of the Nobska steam whistle, announcing her arrival in harbor, two or three times a day in Summer and once or twice daily in the Winter, with her bonus, echoing blasts when she departed. That whistle was deep, low and high-pitched all at the same time and when the ship's mate gave an extra long blast, it was the best sound anywhere! Nothing beat it and the modern air horns on the boats today, can't begin to compare.

Between the town clock's scheduled chimings and the Nobska whistle, we could tell time closely enough, without needing a watch. If we weren't home from school before that 3:00 p.m. blast, we knew we were in for it, for 'dilly-dallying' all the short way from Academy Hill to Willard Street. It was a sound we loved into adulthood, until the Nobska went out of commission and we regretted it for many, many years.

It was a great, wonderful surprise to me and many others that some caring islanders were able to salvage the old steam-powered whistle and install it on the Eagle several years back now. I was walking out of the NHA offices one afternoon at 5:00 and halted dead in my steps when I heard it blowing the longest, sweetest whistle ever, and thought I'd been yanked back into a time-warp! I heard it and still doubted it was what I was hearing. The next day I found out what had happened, jumped into my car at 5:10, drove to Our Island Home and got my Dad walking as quickly as possible to the North window. I opened the oversized pane with under a minute to spare, while he wondered what in the heck I was doing. I just said "Shhh... wait a minute. You'll see!" and then she blew, an even longer, sweeter blast than I'd heard before. I watched my father's eyes open wide and then narrow, like he questioned what he was hearing, even as I had done the day before.

"What the ... the Nobska?" he asked. I told him what I'd learned and we both sat quietly, grins on our faces as we watched, not the modern fat Eagle, but the old stately and slender Nobska sailing out, around the Point.

# Beach Walk

By Julianne Kever

The crisp thin shell of sand breaks with a low crunch on each step
    along the curved shoreline.
I try not to notice the small stones and wavy shells within my reach,
    determined I won't fill my pockets with any more treasures.

I look ahead at a lone gull, bobbing on the bay's gentle undulations
    and marvel at its ability to ride that cold winter water
in feathers, no extra coat like I wear
    against the January chill.

The air is sweet and salt, its own crispness playing at my face,
    the only exposed skin I offer on this cold day.
I am really glad there is no strong breeze to drive me back.

# I Gasp

### By Julianne Kever

I gasp!
...seeing you
before you see me approaching.

Or did you really espy me first,
while I thought I was so stealthily
wending toward you under cover,
of gray-green shadows of the night sentinels?

You stay just out of reach...
typical!
Aloof, yet brazen enough to want
to catch the eye of an admirer,
with your golden arc of broken light!

## 2. ISLAND OF MANY LANDS

**By Joanna Z. Greenfield**

I wish there was someone who could tell me where the stones came from. One can just barely see bits of the world in them, fragments of an ancient volcano trapped in red ice, quartz with twists of iron in it, an agate washed from some river, and granite that could be from any land. A scientist could tell the patterns of the waves, and the stories of the storms from them. What cataclysm could wash the agates from a shallow stream out so deep into the ocean that they never settled to the ground again? Until here.

The stones of 'Sconset come from a different earth than those of Surfside. In my home there are dozens of pink stones, and bright green. Here they are purple and gray and iron and quartzes of all colors. On both beaches, all the rocks are gemstones reflecting light while still on the silk of the sand.

In Concord, a naturalist had led us on tours with the same heartbroken joy for the animals and plants that Thoreau himself had felt. She told us the difference between the edible Queen Anne's lace and its poisonous mimic. It cups itself inward. You can see dew in the bowl in the morning, and snow in the fall. A white cup holding white flakes into the sun. The forest was a museum of great works of art to her, and to me. These rocks would be the same, untainted by pesticides.

The rocks on 'Sconset beach wash in from all over the world, from the depths of the oceans, and from the heights of the mountains, because all land is returning to the sea. Except these little excerpts from the beginning of time. Why doesn't anyone take these rocks? Purple and green, marked with fossils or ancient calcites, or pocked with swirls of lost stone where a softer chemical had washed away, they glint in the sun like rubies and lavender.

The month past, after I'd moved into my winter rental, I tried to fill its barren picture hooks with prints from the thrift shops or the dump. But I couldn't bear to give it all away again in June or live with the weight of more possessions in storage on my soul. One morning, standing barefoot on the empty beach between two dancing dogs, I picked up a shell and looked at the sun through its thin, striated, curve and thought how beautiful it was and how honorably made. Walking home from Surfside with pockets full and sagging, I hung one white shell from each hook, and three bunches of purple everlasting flowers from one bouquet I'd bought from Pumpkin Pond Farm. And in each room I filled a bowl with stones from the sea and put them where they'd catch the light. When I left for my next unknown place, I could empty them all into the driveway and leave, free, unencumbered, but somehow accompanied by the wind and air and salt.

When my home was complete, I held Guppy up toward the mirror, one hand on his curved back, one under his chest. His huge, heavy paws drooped down like an old woman's holding her purse with both wrists bent. His shiny head tucked under mine, he half shut his eyes in unbearable bliss, and dripped from my hands, limp and still. Every now and then a tongue as wide and long as his neck flicked out and curled independently of his body onto my neck. He will be a baby forever, growing up locked in the basement with a dog as gentle and maternal as Mae Mae. She still licks his behind if he cries while he's using the facilities, though she'll do the same to any dog she meets at the park, to their surprise.

Guppy's eyes, staring into the distance with the pain of ecstasy, are as soft and lighted as those of a horse in a Stubb's painting. He was terrified for the first year when I picked him up like this, though so desperate for love and touch in every other way. I think the evil former dog owner must have picked him up and thrown him down the basement stairs when he jumped on her with his sharp, desperate claws. He still screams a sharp yip of fright when someone picks him up by the armpits - because he looks so much like a human baby - as if his doom is upon him. And when I pick him up, carefully, one hand under his bottom, and one on his chest, he still leaps high in the air when I say "up" and has sometimes spilled out of my hands onto his face on the floor.

But this time he rose into the air with me, still and unmoving, and tucked his round, silky head under my chin and breathed out with ecstasy. Even his jowls relaxed, sagging down in soft, white curves. He licked my chin and cheek, bottom half relaxed into me and top half taut with the stretch upward to my face. I told him he was my good boy and he stiffened with pleasure, as if the basement and the angry foot were still in the front of his mind, and I, the present, was still the future, and a dream of a home. Mae Mae has still not learned to trust, though she too drips from my arms when I pick her up. She falls asleep almost instantly with her head pressed into my shoulder, golden ear beneath my chin, but even in her sleep she is holding on, one leg wrapped around my shoulder, the other on my arm holding tight, as if I will lower her from my arms to the basement again, from future to past.

After all my travels, in Africa and across this country, I had been looking for a house to buy, on an island that could disappear in an instant, thirty miles out to sea, far beyond help. The wind blows here all the time, sometimes cold, sometimes warm, on the same day, but sometimes it smells of salt marshes and dried grasses, and wild roses. It was the only place where I could smell the wind.

I stood at the junction between main room and bedroom in front of the mirror and held the black and white ball of silk and satin as if it was I who was being held above a ladder into a basement of unknown depth, to disappear into the dark of the past, as if past were future and I had been the one held in the basement while I grew from puppy to leggy grown up, to desperate, climbing creature. How do you trust a world of toxic food and pesticides and bombs and cleaning supplies that burn children's lungs, and make toddlers run screaming in circles with the pain of a world that smells like evil? Guppy's tongue, wide and long, shot out and lapped my cheek before I could duck, leaving a sticky trail of saliva.

In a bowl on the kitchen table across from us lay quartz and granite and fossils trapped in ancient clay, and agate and mica. There was sun and earth and salt in my house.

"You have mercury poisoning," the doctor had said before I left on my wild fling across the country, that had ended in Nantucket.

I looked at her for a few seconds. I didn't know whether this was another guess spoken like truth, or whether it was some fresh disaster added to the rest, and if my mother was crying because this was bad and she somehow knew it, or happy because we had an answer. She'd been crying a lot lately. That's how she had gotten me out of bed to visit one last doctor. "No," I had said, and she sat by the bed and cried angry tears until I said I'd go.

"You have mercury poisoning," the doctor said, as soon as she saw me but she didn't explain. Then later, "did you work in a factory, at a farm, live in an apartment near a restaurant?"

"No to all," I said. I'd never worked as anything but an anthropologist and a temp secretary. I lived in an apartment over a bar in graduate school, but they didn't really serve food. At least I didn't think they actually cooked anything they served.

She wrote something in her notes, already pages long. But all the doctors had written pages and then told me I was imagining the illness or it was psychological or I needed sinus surgery because that was what they did, or my thyroid removed because that was what they did.

"Did you ever work in a stable?" she asked, and my mother and I stopped looking hypnotized at the upside down scrawls and stared at her.

"Yes."

"Okay. The apartment probably sprayed pesticides twice a month prophylactically for cockroaches. Many buildings do even if they're not near a food source because they don't want to be sued. Pesticides usually have mercury in them. Hay for horses is sprayed with mercury so the farmers don't have to have three dry days before and after haying. Mercury is an anti-fungal."

She whipped out a stack of blank paper. For the next ten minutes my mother and I watched her draw chemical formulae faster than she'd written in my chart, one line after another. We craned our heads to watch her write as if we'd understand them if we looked closer. Finally, she asked us for the third time if we understood, looked at our faces, sighed, and stopped in mid formula. Resigned to human limitations, she handed me the stack, grabbed it back again and wrote incomprehensible summaries and explanations on each page, handed me the stack again, then snatched it back for a few more words and arrows pointing to different lines.

"Do you have any questions?" she asked in the dull voice of someone who thinks so much above ordinary humans that she finds us mysterious in our thoughts.

"Um." I wanted to ask her a question about the formulae she was so excited about because I was afraid that this was all I was going to get but I couldn't remember anything she'd said.

"Does this mean I have multiple sclerosis and mercury poisoning too?"

"No no." She flicked the papers out of my limp hands and wrote again furiously. She looked up at us to explain, sighed again and returned to human speech. "You don't have MS. There's nothing wrong with you. I told you when you walked in that you had mercury poisoning because your eyelid was flickering. MS makes your thumbs flicker like Parkinson's." She grabbed the papers again and showed us I think what the two diseases do to your brain and then what the mercury had done to mine.

She slapped the papers down on the desk, within easy reach of her pen. "Do you have any more questions?"

We listened to the clock tick. My mother leaned forward. "Um. What do we do about it?"

She flipped to the second page and pointed at three formulae and explained them again.

"I mean what can we do to get this out of her body?"

She pointed at one of the equations. Chelation therapy. "Normally I'd give pills but you're at risk of seizures. Two weeks of IV chelation should do it. And then of course you'll have to avoid mercury for the rest of your life. You'll be sensitive to it." She banged open a drawer and pulled out another stack of papers. We flinched but these were typed lists. Small font on both sides of the paper, small margins, and no spaces, the opposite of all the term papers I'd written at the last minute. "Avoid these things, and any pesticides."

Hundreds and hundreds of household supplies. Sponges, anti microbial soap, shower curtains, fertilizer, and on and on and on.

I was afraid of the chelation therapy, my body was so fragile it felt as if one more chemical would throw it over some invisible edge. But she injected calcium and magnesium first, to protect my heart and instantly I was flooded with breath. I was all right again. Day after day I did the IV therapy and the tremors subsided to a flicker, then an invisible twitch, then nothing. My death sentence had lifted.

I put the papers the doctor had given me in a drawer in a desk because I was more afraid to learn how little I could trust the world in which I lived, than I was to breathe in the poison again.

For six years after the chelation therapy, I had run across the country from one hostel or camp site to another, driven away from each by chemicals and unbreathable air, because I thought we should live with joy. Like the animals we used to be, we should eat fruit from the tree, tomatoes from the ground, water from a stream, and sleep in the sun and breathe clean air.

In that wild dash across the country, I lived in a tent by the beach in Sanibel Island, surrounded by rescued parrots, in a cabin hostel in the Sandia mountains with six donkeys, in a fisherman's shack in an artists' colony, in a two hundred year old house by a ski resort. I sat with a coyote teacher among the Petroglyphs of half his ancestors, and swam in hot springs with tropical fish. A friend let me sleep in his woods and a bear came every morning to smell the base of the tent, while my dogs lay rigid and nonchalant against me.

It was one magic moment after another, except that in each place I lived, children were dying.

I was sprayed with pesticides in Florida, I swam with benzene in Vermont, I was sprayed for bed bugs in New Hampshire, I smelled the smoke of burning factories in a forest fire in the mountains of New Mexico, I breathed the smog of Los Angeles in the tiny town of Cambria, and the mercury of battery factories in Connecticut. In each town there were jars on the counters of gas stations and general stores. There was a picture of a child on each jar, usually bald, wearing a bright bed jacket or hospital gown, with the slogan please give, Kathleen needs money for her next surgery, As if this has become normal, the way life was, that there was no connection between the fracking for gas, the paper mill, the computer keyboard factory that dumped arsenic in the water. I felt as if I was the only person who saw the line between the chemicals and the children lying in the hospital bed. Some people fought, but they were not heard. We have lost the right to life, not because of the freedom to choose, but because our air, our water, our land, and our food are being harvested and sold to people who already own a dozen castles.

I spiraled back to Nantucket, over and over again until I came to rest here, in the place in my country that was the most like Africa. Here too, were lighted grasses bent in a wind of sweet dust and sun. And people who lived in the water, on the water, on the land, on the roofs. I will never really leave Africa, no matter how far I go from it, but I can sleep at night here, and listen to things older than the earth.

## 3. GHOSTS OF 'SCONSET

**By Daryl Westbrook**

The village of Siasconset was initially developed by wealthy mid-westerners who built large homes overlooking the Ocean. The immediate charm of the village delighted them. The village was quaint, relaxing and offered an ocean breeze.

It was Ed Underhill, a writer for the *New York Tribune*, who conceived that the oddity and novelty of the fishing cottages in the village, if duplicated, would be of great appeal to the visitors of 'Sconset, as it's known locally. His vision was to create their piquant and engaging look and make them available for rent.

He bought up land and built small cottages covering their front porches with lovely roses, which appealed immediately to actors and actresses who were looking for something affordable away from the heat and the boredom of New York in the summer. In no time these porches became small stages for the actors and actresses who discovered 'Sconset. The appeal to the Broadway contingent, besides the escape from the heat of the city when the theatres closed, was the small village that offered a less restrictive social experience. With the advent of the train service to 'Sconset, it became easy for them to get to this small out of the way destination.

Imagine the excitement of the train ride along the ocean bluff past Tom Nevers looking to the North over sheep pastures and spotting Sankaty Head Light House in the distance, carrying them down the hill into Codfish Park and the ocean side station. A short distance from the station were cabanas for beach goers to change into their bathing attire should they be in 'Sconset for only the day. Horse and carriages awaited those visitors who were staying at one of the hotels, Atlantic House or Ocean House, or at a rented cottage. The advertisements drew visitors to 'Sconset as they depicted the seaside setting overlooking the Atlantic, a distance from the Town, where the air is pure right off the ocean and one could enjoy the unadulterated sea breeze.

Some 200 theatrical persons visited 'Sconset during the late 1800s through the early 1920s before Hollywood introduced the speaking pictures that attracted them to the west coast. The village had enchanted some who continued to summer in the village and eventually built or bought a home. Generations of these families returned every summer, enjoying the tradition of their summer home and renewing summer friendships.

I can remember as a child some of the actors, but mostly I remember the music. Windows were often open and one could hear a song being sung or played on a piano. My most vivid memory was of band leader who lived in the heart of the village. He would play the Big Band sounds whenever the spirit moved him, morning, noon or night on his piano or record player that he brought with him every summer. If a well-known musician died during the year, he would organize his recordings of the artist's music and play a tribute to him. This musical obituary would be anticipated throughout the village.

The *Inquirer and Mirror* had a column in the paper called the "'Sconset Note's" which let everyone know the happenings in 'Sconset. It was a gossip column of sorts. The Hedda Hopper of 'Sconset was a bit of a sleuth. Many wanted to avoid being mentioned, but she was vigilant if she got wind of a good bit of news whatever that might be.

As a columnist, she loved rubbing shoulders with the theatrical crowd and was always reporting the latest stage reviews and kudos. John Steinbeck often visited 'Sconset and was known for the famous guests he entertained;, the guests were always mentioned in the column. The 'Sconset Notes were a fun read because they were newsy and a bit tongue and cheek. They bring to mind one such visitor who wanted to remain unknown during his stay in 'Sconset and was quite concerned that his presence would be leaked to the newspapers. Many assurances were given that no one would be told that he had rented a house in 'Sconset for the month. At the end of his stay, he was questioned as to whether he felt his stay was kept confidential and as restful as he had hoped. He replied that he was so anonymous that he almost took guitar in hand and performed at the market to get anyone to recognize him.

Wade Cottage, which was known as an Inn as well as for the cottages, often attracted high profile personalities, who graced the "'Sconset Notes" column. A grand piano was in the great room and was often the center of entertainment for one or more virtuosos. The aforementioned band leader, was one of the frequent guests, who tickled the ivories. It never occurred to me back in those days, if guests might have wanted to sleep in the rooms above, when piano and songs were played into the early hours of the morning. My mother had sung professionally and was a frequent guest at that piano, which is why I can attest to the late night hour of the entertainment.

With such a history of the theatre in 'Sconset, it would not be surprising to see the ghosts of the theatrical set who wandered the shell clad streets in robes and turbans going to the beach return to the village. In the early morning mist of 2000, however, it is not ghosts walking or riding their bikes through 'Sconset.

It is the quadrille of Esther William's wannabes who appear for their morning swim in season. The ladies appear in white terrycloth robes, some with hoods, others with turbans, strolling forth from behind their perfectly pruned hedges for the pool. They cavort in unison doing their aerobics, which in jest dubs them the Esther Williams quadrille. It is from behind the hedges of one of the houses that a theatre person had built that one of the ladies emerges. Most of the women have grown up or married and raised their children in 'Sconset. For them, 'Sconset is a safe haven away from the formality of their real world off-island where propriety would demand a different standard as wives of diplomats, lawyers themselves and society mavens. Their comfort level comes from a deep friendship of knowing each other for so long, which is evident in their interactions.

These ladies of the morning mist inspire one to think of that past when cabanas lined the beach. The actors and actresses left their cottages and strolled to the ocean without concern. They had come to escape their celebrity hood. If the ghosts' spirits still linger in 'Sconset, which is possible. I am delighted that the goings on have not changed that much.

This all brings to mind a stanza of a song from On The Isle, "a place to spend the summer in some style, pack your bag, board the ship you're sure to have a happy trip so hustle down for a while. It's very gay in every way, we never work when we can play."

Generations have sung those words. Today life is not any different than when the song was written or the Broadway Players were in action on the stage of the SiaSconset Casino.

Nantucket Atheneum Writer's Group

## Summer

**by Ursula Austin**

Tender under heat
willows force a wow
as birds concede
every evenings eve
precious singing deep
soft while humans sleep

## The Pond

**by Ursula Austin**

Sesachacha
pearly sheet deposited
in the middle of Blue Black Verdancy.
Celebrated in haunting song
of night cicada's rustling.
Terraced skies with
promised thunderstorms.
Animal shadows lingering
in mystery of stillness
as closer to town
Brightly lit Orange windows
aspire to nature's painting
Lost in the glaring
Hiss of moving car tangos.

# 4. COMING OF AGE

**By Terry L. Norton**

Little Lily, that's what she had been called, but she wasn't little anymore. She was 15, almost a grown woman, out of short skirts; but she was a young woman in a quandary. Six weeks ago, while plowing the fields, her father had dropped dead leaving a widow and seven children. Lily was the eldest; the youngest was 8 months. It was also the day that the wind went out of her mother's sails, so to speak.

The day her father died was the first nice weather after a long sedentary winter. He had been eager to start work on the field. Joshua would normally have been on the plowshare helping his father as Lily kept the cantankerous mule moving forward; but Joshua had gone over to the Lewis farm to help sheer sheep. Not a couple of hours into the job of plowing, her father made a strange noise. She looked back to see his lips were blue and his face a strange pallor, then he crumpled.

The memory of the funeral rushed back unbidden: the family all in black, her father's coffin on a bier on the altar, the church was filled to overflowing, sobbing uncontrollably. She remembered the minister calling upon his congregation to remember the many times Tristram Gardner had helped his friends, neighbors, and fellow islanders that no one would feel the pangs of hunger or the chill of a Nor'easter and to remember Mr. Gardner's grieving family. Obed Lewis, their neighbor, had delivered the eulogy and spoke about how the Island had lost a fine man who set an example for the younger generation.

When the family returned to the house that day and after all the condolences made, her mother took to her bed. Lily wished she had been able to take to her bed.

She shook her head to dispel the memory. She wanted to remember how when she and Joshua and their father were working the fields, her mother would come out at midday and bring them bread hot from the oven to eat with fresh churned butter. Lydia at 12 stayed home and help Mother with the little ones: Amelie 8, Phineas 6, Alicia 4 and "the Boy" baby Zebulon.

The fields had stood fallow since her father's death. Her mother wouldn't allow anyone to go near them; some nonsense about dying there as well. Lily had no uncles to go to. Her father's youngest brother was still at sea on the Whaler Christopher Mitchell and his other brother had died of Cholera four years ago. Her aunt was married to a light-house keeper on the mainland.

Mother was an off-islander; her family lived on the mainland 30 miles across the water. There seemed to be no one to whom Lily could turn for help.

She stood ankle deep in water looking west toward town and the tall ships in the harbor. She was worried. The food stuffs were running out and without an income, there would be no way to buy what they needed.

Way out here in Polpis, people didn't just drop by. The farms out here were isolated. This was the time of year when all the farmers were busy getting in their fields. Her father used to go help and they in turn would help him get the fields ready. She hadn't been able to help anyone as her father had. As for someone from town dropping, they might if on a rantum scoot but that was about it. If her family lived in Town, people would have dropped in regularly to check on them, especially the church ladies. But not out here. Mother hadn't even left the farm to go to church since the funeral. She hardly left her room.

She glanced up at a seagull as it flew up and up then dropped a crab on the sand to crack the shell. She watched it dive right behind the falling crustacean to grab it before another gull shot in to steal its prize. She envied seagulls: to be able to fly away from trouble and just find what they needed. Lily picked up a scallop shell and skipped it across the lazy waves watching the droplets it kicked up sparkle and glint in the sun.

At a shout from toward Cotue, she waved at a dory of fishermen pulling for home; they would have dragged the boat from the ocean into the harbor at the haul-over on Great Point at the end of the harbor. They waved and actually turned in toward her.

Mr. Asa Whitney climbed out carrying a bluefish. "Sorry to hear about Tris, your pa. How's your ma?" He held the fish out by the gills.

Lily shrugged, "Not good." She took the fish he offered. "Thank you."

Asa Whitney was a big, barrel-chested beast of a man with a thick beard and shock of dark hair speckled with grey. He used to be a whaler until the ship he was on sank off Otaheito in a storm. A week drifting in a boat seemed to sour him to that lifestyle. Now he was a simple fisherman with a wife and children. He lived south of town near the Creeks.

"Ain't been to church," he noted.

Lily shook her head and shrugged again. She dug her toe into the wet sea bed feeling ashamed. She didn't know how to tell him about her mother giving up.

Asa patted her tiny shoulder with his maw of a hand. "Not healthy, nope. Not healthy." He returned to the dory and his friends and pushed them back to deep water as he lumbered into the boat. It heeled precariously under his prodigious weight but quickly settled and the three men started hauling for home again.

Lily turned from the water, climbed the bluff that was Polpis Head and started home; she had an eight-pound fish to fillet. This would feed the family, and it was mighty generous of Mr. Whitney to give it over like he did. Lily would have to think of a way to repay him.

Barefoot she walked the sand tracks left by wagons that had traveled from the Polpis Road out to the point. Beach plum, low-bush blueberrys, bay berry and winterberry grew along the road and across the moors. If she looked south, she could see the Sankaty Light. If she looked north, she could see the Great Point Light. If she looked west, she could see the church spires in town. The sun was warm but not at full summer strength. Late April could be fickle on the Island. She was lucky it happened to be warm. She cut across the field where the sheep, two family cows and their mule grazed.

The house had been built by her grandfather. Over the years as first his family then her father's family grew, it had been added onto. It started out as a simple saltbox with the kitchen sitting room and sleeping area all as one and a loft; but now it was a proper two-stories with a porch across the front. There were two extensions off the back. Her grandfather built the first to be the master bedroom when her father and his brothers and his sister got too old to share the loft; her aunt had slept in the front room. When he married, her father had turned his parents' bedroom into a sitting room with book shelves and built the second addition as a bedroom and nursery for him and his wife. When Joshua was born, he raised the roof and made two bedrooms on the second floor: one for the boys and one for the girls. The main chimney ran up the very center of the house with four fireplaces: the kitchen, sitting room and each upstairs bedroom. Her parents' bedroom and nursery had its own fire place.

## The Moving Pen

Joshua was sitting on the porch watching an ant war. She remembered something her teacher said at school about how strong ants were compared to their tiny size. She wished she had such an army to help her now.

When Joshua heard his big sister's foot falls he looked up. "Where'd the fish come from?"

"Mr. Whitney. Fetch a knife." She flopped the fish onto the porch floor boards and sat down. When Joshua returned, she started to work on the fish. "Bring me a plate and water jug." First she scraped the scales off as best she could. Next she cut the head off right behind the gills then slit the fish down its belly then up the spine going around the dorsal fin. Lastly, she separated the tail.

Joshua set the plate next to her and rinsed off the work area with water from the jug. She handed him the fish head, "for crabbing." She pulled the insides out then began peeling the meat off trying to avoid as many of the tiny bones as possible. When she finished, she had two sizeable fillets and her hands, apron and porch covered with fish guts and blood.

"Where's Ma?" She asked standing and picking up the plate.

"In bed," Joshua said. "Got one of her headaches again."

Lily sighed. Her mother was always in bed these days. If it wasn't a headache, it was some other malady that afflicted the woman. As the eldest, it fell upon her to take care of her siblings and her grieving mother. She had not been able to go back to school. Resentment threatened to engulf her; she kicked the door jamb to vent. She would be cooking dinner again. "Clean up the mess, would you?"

"Can I go crabbing if I do?" Joshua asked.

"Yep, tomorrow. You can catch tomorrow's supper." She would have roughed his hair but her hands were nasty dirty. "Lydia," she called.

Lydia was all legs and arms and no substance. She came in with The Boy on her hip. "What?" Her eyes popped. "Oh, goody."

"We got any to eat with this?" Lily asked.

"Phineas, go to the root cellar and see what we got." Lydia relayed. She bounced the restless infant on her hip. "I'm worried for The Boy. I think he's got a fever."

"And Ma?"

"She's down with the vapors or something." With one hand Lydia got down a grilling pan and set it on the stove. "I tried to get her to help me with The Boy, but," she trailed off.

Lily groaned. "We got to do something. We got to get crops planted, we got to get something to sell to the ship masters and to put up for next winter. Has the cow been milked?"

Lydia nodded, "Amelie did it. Can we send Joshua for the doctor?"

Lily nodded. "Tell him to take the mule."

"But Ma said. . ."

"I don't give a care about what Ma said. She don't give a care about us or she'd be standing here grilling this fish and tending her Boy while we took care of the fields!" Lily exploded and burst into tears.

Lydia silently slipped out to pass the instructions to Joshua. "And be careful," she admonished him.

Lily had to work at not taking her frustration out on the fish, but she couldn't control the tears. She wiped her eyes with her sleeve and snuffled. Dear God she missed her father. Why did he have to die on them like that? It wasn't fair. The school teacher had told her she was smart enough to become a teacher herself, but she had to quit school to take care of her family after Pa died. And why did Ma have to be so-so-so selfish? Did she think that she could give up on her children with her husband gone? What would Pa say to her?

"Lil?" A plaintive voice pulled her out of her train of thought.

She turned to see Phineas' curly brown hair and green eyes peaking cautiously around the door jamb. She wiped her eyes and sniffed one last time then smiled. "Hi Phin." She heard the hoof beats of the mule leaving.

"I brunged a onion and corn." He held out the jar of canned corn from last fall and the onion.

Lily nodded and took them. "Thank you, Phin." It wasn't what she would have picked out but when you sent an unsupervised six-year-old to do a job, you didn't complain about the results. She'd figure out something.

"Is The Boy gonna die?" He jerked a fat little thumb toward town where Joshua was headed.

"No, it's not serious. Babies get sick." She explained hoping she was right. "Doc'll put him right."

"How we gonna pay the doctor?" Phineas asked.

Lily's stomach dropped. She felt the tears starting to return and shook her head daring not to speak.

"Where's the mule going? We need the mule here. What if something happens?" The panicked voice of their mother shook the rafters. She was headed for the kitchen.

"Go to Lydia," Lily ordered Phineas pushing him toward the door.

If she hadn't come from her bedroom, Lily would have been hard pressed to recognize her mother. The once robust cheery woman with the peaches and cream complexion and lush brown hair was now a pale, pasty haunt with sunken eyes and a dark tangled mass in stark relief to the pallor. "You little witch, how could you let the mule run off?"

"Didn't run off. Sent Josh for the doctor," Lily tried to explain reasonably.

The sunken eyes opened even wider in horror. "How dare you endanger my precious child that way."

Lily saw her mother raise her hand to strike. She was faster and her mother reeled at the unexpected shock of the blow. "Shut up!" Lily howled into her mother's face. She suddenly realized that she was the same height as her mother. "How dare you endanger all of us by …" words failed her. "Go back to bed you lazy bug." She turned her attention back to the fish taking it off the grill before it over cooked. "Let me work. Go! Get!" she shouted into her mother's face.

Stunned, her mother backed away then meekly turned and disappeared into the bowels of the house.

# The Moving Pen

What had she done? Lily was horrified at how she had treated her mother. "Oh, God forgive me," she whimpered and sagged to the floor sobbing. She became aware of bodies around her and hands touching her. Lydia, Amelie, Phineas and Alicia were on the floor beside her.

Alicia crawled into her lap and put her arms around Lily's neck. "I love you."

Lily hugged her baby sister fiercely, "I love you too." She took a deep breath. "You'll be all right. I'll take care of you." She cried and they cried with her.

It was a couple of hours before Joshua returned with the doctor. It was late, but Lily had kept some of the fish and onion-corn mix hot for him.

Lydia stood by and answered questions as the doctor examined the infant. Lydia had always helped their mother with the younger children so it had been natural for her to keep doing that after their mother abdicated her responsibilities.

"It is nothing more than his first teeth coming in," the doctor announced. "He'll run a low fever but it won't mean a thing. He will be fussy; give him something hard to chew on like a carrot. How are the rest of you?" he asked.

The children all assured him that they were hale and hearty.

"I got a new toof," Phineas showed him proudly.

He patted the boy's head. "Where's Mrs. Gardner?" He asked.

"Her room," Lily explained. He indicated she come with him and headed back to see their mother.

She picked up a hurricane lamp and brought it along. "She doesn't get up much, stays to her room."

The doctor wrinkled his nose when he opened the door. There were no candles or lamps and all the windows were shut and curtains drawn; he immediately began opening the windows to air out the stale smell of unwash. He stood over the children's mother tsking and shook his head.

"I am going to need more light." He told Lily.

"Amelie, bring two more lamps." She set the lamp she had brought on the bedside table.

The despondent widow lay in her bed fully clothed with the bed covers up around her chin not meeting the doctor's eyes. Lily was ashamed for her.

"What happened to your cheek, Mrs. Gardner?" The doctor asked in a loud voice as if Mrs. Gardner were hard of hearing.

"I slapped her," Lily admitted. "I'm a wretched child."

"Why did you slap your mother?" he asked.

Lily was surprised by the lack of scolding in his tone. She told him about her tantrum that afternoon.

"When was the last time she ate?"

"She ate some fish."

"When was the last time she bathed?"

"Pa's funeral."

"Mrs. Gardner, I am going to examine you," he announced again in a loud clear voice.

Lily figured he was just trying to get through to her. "She has terrible headaches that make her sick."

"When did those headaches start?" The doctor took the woman's face in his hand and turned her to look at him.

"After Pa died."

The doctor lifted the lamp and studied Mrs. Gardner's eyes. The woman flinched at the bright light. "Is she nursing the baby?"

"No, sir. Lydia gives him cow's milk."

He felt around the jaw and neck and pressed on her stomach without moving the bedcovers. Mrs. Gardner didn't move the whole time he poked and prodded her. He listened to her heart. At last he stood shaking his head.

"I can't find anything physically wrong." He again spoke loudly. "Mrs. Gardner, I know you're grieving but you have children to take care of. This selfish nonsense must stop. What would Mr. Gardner say if he saw you acting this way?"

The only response he got was a whimper and the woman rolled over and curled up.

"If this doesn't stop, I'll have to have her committed."

"No, I'll take care of her. I promise," Lily begged suddenly frightened. "I won't hit her again."

He lay his hand against her cheek. "You shouldn't be taking care of her. She should be taking care of herself and the little ones, so you, Lydia, and Josh can go back to school." He turned and left the room.

"Uh, Doctor Coleman, I don't have any money," Lily finally admitted to his back.

He grunted with a shrug. "Not to worry. We take care of each other here, not like on the mainland." At the front door he turned back. "I'll be back in a couple of days to check on the lot of you. We'll figure something out for payment. Good night." He put his hat on and disappeared into the dark of the night.

The kitchen was cleaned up, the little ones were in bed, and Lydia was soothing the fussy baby. Lily went out into the yard and stared up at the mass of stars overhead. "Pa, help me. What do I do?" She began walking and her feet led her to the fallow field. She squatted and scooped up a handful of the rich course soil feeling the weight of its moisture. There was still time to get a crop in, but she had no idea how she and Joshua would do that alone. "We have to try."

She returned to the house and made her way to bed. She didn't sleep. She lay there turning things over and over in her head. It was up to her to save this family.

"Joshua, you harness up the mule when you're done," she told her brother at breakfast. "Amelie, I need you to feed the animals. Can you do it alone?" That had been Lily's chore, but today she had to get to work on the field.

The eight-year-old nodded.

"That's your job today, after milking the cow. Lydia, you have your hands full, but if you think you can do it, try to get Ma out of those clothes and bathed. I won't be bothered if you can't. We can worry about her another day. Phineas, you come with Joshua and me. You need to lead the mule."

The little boy's eyes widened and he puffed his chest. That was important work.

The plowshare was where it had been left after her father collapsed. She and Joshua hooked up the mule and with prodding from the six-year-old, the mule started moving. Lily and Joshua wrestled the plowshare. It was very slow going and the furrows weren't as neat as her father's but they were getting something done.

At midday, Lydia called them over. She had a picnic basket with milk, fresh bread, and honey. "I got Ma at the butter churn, but don't know for how long. She washed her face but I couldn't get her to change her clothes." She studied how much they had gotten done. "Well, we might have enough for the family."

"Where'd you find honey?" Lily asked.

"Amelie found a hive in an old scrub oak. Lily, we need staples something bad." Lydia bounced the now every-present baby on her hip. She held a carrot for him to gum, and he seemed very much content.

"But we don't have any cash." Lily heaved a sigh as she wracked her brain for anything that could be used to buy the things they needed. "Joshua, why don't you and Phineas take that fish head and go crabbing then maybe see if you can find some Quahogs."

"What about the field?" Joshua asked.

"We'll get back to that after the tide turns. First, get us something for supper tonight." Lily was loath to slaughter any of the farm animals; the sheep's wool, meat from piglets and chicken eggs would be needed later and could be sold.

The two boys whooped and took off running.

"Look, there's Mr. Lewis," Lydia pointed and waved at the man crossing the field.

"Ladies," he greeted as if neither of them was in short skirts.

"Good day, Mr. Lewis," the two girls responded.

"Came to check on you," Mr. Lewis looked over the erratic fresh furrows with an intense blue-eyed gaze. "Looks like a mite of trouble there." He was a very tall, thin man with big hands and gaunt features but his mouth was turned up in a perpetual grin. His hair was mostly white now.

Lily had heard some of the older women say that he had been a head turner in his younger days. She thought he was still handsome, for an old man. "It's hard without Pa," She admitted.

He looked at her muddy boots and the dirt at the hem of her skirt. "Looks like you could use some help."

"Can't afford to pay," she said.

"That's what neighbors are for," he said still looking over the unfinished field.

"I better get back to the house. It was nice seeing you, Mr. Lewis," Lydia picked up the basket and left.

Mr. Lewis folded his hands behind his back and surveyed the situation. "Yep, need some help. Well, it was nice seeing you Miss Gardner."

"Good day, Mr. Lewis. Mr. Lewis, do you know anyone hiring? I work hard."

The older man pursed his lips and thought long and hard. He slowly shook his head. "Can't think of anyone. Sides, who would take care of your family if you leave?" He tipped his hat and headed back across the field towards his farm.

Lily leaned against the grazing mule and swore very quietly to herself. He was right. Who would take care of the family and the farm? They needed every able-bodied member here, working in order to survive.

She led the mule back to the house and turned it out. "Lydia, what do we need?"

"Sugar, flour, salt, lamp oil, tea would be nice." Lydia studied her sister. "You going to town?"

"Maybe the grocer will give me credit like he did Pa." Lily headed up to her room to clean up and change. When she came back down she told Lydia she was leaving the mule in case of an emergency. She picked up a basket and headed out the door.

It was several miles to town along the road. Luckily, Mr. Lewis came along with his wagon and gave her ride. Neither said anything along the way which suited Lily. She tried to enjoy the early spring day, the warm sun and singing birds. She felt like she hadn't heard bird song in years.

At the bottom of Main Street, she thanked Mr. Lewis and climbed down. He was headed out onto to Straight Wharf to deliver produce to a whaling ship stocking up for its next voyage. Main Street sloped up between Mr. Rotch's counting house and the Pacific Bank, the only two brick buildings on the street. She was about to turn into the grocers when she met the Congregational minister.

"Miss Gardner," he greeted.

"Reverend," she answered with a curtsy.

"You're family hasn't been to church," he noted in his stern sermon voice.

"No, Sir." She thought fast. "Ma hasn't been well." It was the truth; she could never lie to a man of the cloth.

"Sorry to hear that. Has the doctor seen her?"

"Yes, Sir," she said.

"Did he say what's the matter?"

She shook her head sadly. How could she tell this man that his mother had abrogated her guardianship of her family? She heard him heave a sigh and looked up.

"I shall see what help I can muster, and I shall pray for all of you," he assured.

"Thank you, Reverend."

He went on his way, and she went into the store. It was busy so she looked around not wanting to air the family troubles in front of people who knew her family so well. She smiled and greeted and accepted condolences as she looked longingly at the penny candy. At last it was just her and the store keeper.

"Good afternoon, Miss Gardner," he greeted. "Your father was a good man. We all miss him. What can I do for you?"

"Thank you, sir. Well, you see," she bit her lip then explained her financial destitution in the face of needs to feed the family. She couldn't look at him as she spoke; somehow it seemed more like she was quietly rehearsing her pitch that way. When she finished, he was silent for an unusually long time.

"I see. Credit you say. Let me check my books." He went into the back room.

She could hear him talking to his wife. She wanted to cry but this wasn't the place.

He came out with a huge grin. "You are in luck, little lady. Your family still has some credit to account. What do you need?"

For the first times in weeks she felt hopeful. She told him the list as Lydia had presented it. "And some tea and maybe canned vegetables would be good if we can afford it."

He gathered the goods to include the tea and several canned beans and a stick of candy for each child. "There, we're even now."

She bit back tears of joy. "Thank you Mr. Caine." She curtsied and with a spring in her step headed out the door. She felt like she could hold her head up in town. She hadn't had to beg after all.

"Lily!" she turned at the deep voice and saw Michael Coffin jog up. He was all of 16 years and over the winter had gone from being shorter than her to taller, though he had not yet filled out. His voice had also dropped to that of a man's. "Lily, guess what?"

She smiled up at him. "What?"

"I'm shipping out with Captain Chase as a deckhand," he was bouncing on his toes. "We leave Saturday. Will you come see me off?"

The two had been friends as long as she could remember. She had always sat across the aisle from him at school. He was the one in class who always got in trouble for disrupting things, but he could make up the most fantastical stories. She loved his stories.

"I got lots of work on the farm, but I'll try."

"Please, it would mean the world to me, and I'll give you a good bye kiss." His blue eyes glinted.

She reached up and tapped his cheek lightly. "Don't you dare, Mr. Coffin." She tried to sound stern and grown up.

"Maybe when I get back I'll ask you to marry me."

"Maybe when you get back, pigs will be flying," she laughed. "Besides I have a farm to take care of."

He snorted. "By then Josh will be old enough to do that, and I'll buy you a fine home here in town with my share."

She shook her head amused. "Mr. Coffin, you are a dreamer."

He turned suddenly serious. "I mean it, Lily, please come see me off?"

She nodded. "I better go." Before she could react, he stole a kiss on her cheek and darted off. She touched the spot where his lips had touched her and watched him. Whaling men died, but . . . She would have a number of years to think about what he had said.

He glanced back over his shoulder and waved. She returned the wave and pointed her nose back to home.

It was nearly time to start supper when she turned off the Polpis Road into the yard. Joshua and Phineas were sitting on the porch with a hammer and chisel working diligently at something. When she got close enough, she could see that they were breaking up Welk and Quahog shells.

"What you doing?" She asked. There were bits of pink, white, and purple shell piled at hand.

"Making Wampum," Joshua announced. "Old Joe showed me how. Maybe we can trade it with the Injuns?"

"Maybe we can. Good thinking. Did you get any crabs?"

Joshua nodded and pointed at a pail from which came scratching noises and she could see a blue claw snapping above the rim. "Did you get stuff?" He looked at the basket.

"Yep." She went in.

"Ma is in a state," Lydia greeted.

"What about?" Lily asked feeling the wind go out of her sails.

Lydia grinned devilishly. "I propped all her windows open and took down the curtains to 'wash them'. I wouldn't let her hid in the dark. Even took the bed linings off to air them out. Then told her she had to use the privy, not the chamber pot."

Lily smiled. "She's got a headache again?"

Lydia shrugged. "Yep, but she can't hide. Oops, The Boy's awake. She's still in her stinky same clothes though."

"We'll tackle that tomorrow," Lily promised. She turned to storing the goods she bought and hid the candy. That would be a surprise after supper tonight.

That evening, they had a meal of steamed crabs and beans with the candy for dessert. The seven children were in good spirits, and they all sat together working on the wampum beads singing songs. Mother had slunk back into the dark of her room and took her meal there, all she ate was one crab leg and a couple of the beans.

"Tomorrow, Joshua, Phineas and I will get back to work on the field. Amelie, do you think you can do the laundry by yourself?"

Amelie nodded.

"Alicia, you will feed the chickens and the pigs."

Alicia nodded eagerly. They handed her random pieces of white shell since she broke more than managed to shape.

"Lydia, please try again to get Ma out of those clothes so they can be washed."

"I'll do my best," Lydia promised.

The next morning, everyone set to their assigned tasks. Lily was back in the field, this time in a pair of her father's old pants. They were way too big, but it was better than soiling her dresses. She and the two boys could actually hear Lydia and their mother having it out about getting out of the clothes. Lily put her back to the plowshare getting better at making straight rows, but it was still slow going. At this rate, it would be July before they were done.

After a bit the shouting at the house ceased and Lily could hear the distant waves breaking on the eastern shore. Song birds were singing, and the gulls were keening over the harbor. It was a cool day but the work was hot.

Suddenly, she heard singing that was not the birds and straightened to listen. It was people singing, a lot of people. She turned and looked down the road. She could see Mr. Whitney, the Doctor and the Congregational minister riding at the head of a column of wagons full of people.

She and her brothers stared confused. This was the middle of the week, not the normal time for a church outing. She spun when Mr. Lewis and his wife hailed her from across the field. Suddenly, the couple and the crowd were converging on the Gardner farm.

"Go greet the Lewises," she urged Joshua. "Stay with the mule," she told Phineas, then broke into a jog back to the house. When she arrived, people were piling out of the wagons laden with supplies and food. Lydia stood on the porch disheveled and as confused as Lily. The grocer and his wife started unloading items of food stuffs, which the ladies from church carried into the house. One took The Boy from Lydia and told the girl to go clean up.

Women were banging about inside, a cadre of cleaners. Ma was weeping as ladies cajoled her. Amelie was relieved of the laundry and urged to go play with children she hadn't seen in weeks. Men were unloading other plowshares by the field and hitching up their own mules and horses.

"What?" Was all Lily could manage looking at Mr. Whitney, the doctor and the minister. The three stood tall and studied her silently for a moment.

"Come to help," Asa said.

"Here to check on you," the doctor said.

The minister lay a hand on her shoulder. "We are Island folk. We help each other. All you had to do was ask."

She hung her head and bit her lip. "Thank you," she felt tears filling her eyes.

Suddenly she was caught up in a bear hug and spun around.

"Michael Coffin," she chastised. "Aren't you supposed to be lading the ship?"

He grinned, "Captain Chase told me to come out and help. He'd be here himself, but he's got work to do. He let five other members of the crew come with me to help." He was still holding her.

"Let go of me you wretch," she ordered.

He shook his head. "When I come back, I'm going to marry you, Lily Gardner. I'm going to be a man of substance and you will wear silks from china and live in a fine big house on Main Street."

She allowed herself to lean against him.

## 4. THE SUMMER PEOPLE

**By Kristine Glazer**

I waited for the last turn of the calendar; so much time from January to June, the final month of school.. My yearning for the ferry, the sea, the sand, the signal, the start of summer, and then, we would depart.

We went from north to south, then east to west, and back again.
We travelled by road, bike, sea and salty air- to the beach, farm, ballet and concerts, too. We combed the sand, wandered the paths, spied hedges, and flowers, the hydrangeas – so blue.

And, suddenly summer was at an end. Our return to highways, trains, and shopping malls, a never-ending parade of super-size retail again.

Then one June, in an afternoon, we left for the summer, autumn, winter, and spring. We stayed long past summer, when the summer people were gone, when the warm sun stayed for a while. We went to our favorite restaurants with no reservations. We found parking with ease and Stop & Shop was a breeze.

I rode my bicycle alone on the path.
I looked for treasures on the beach, with no one in sight.
Then it was winter, and I listened to the wind.
I watched the birds atop the wire, not three, not four, but many more.

# The Moving Pen

I saw stars that stayed, high in the clear night sky.
I found friends through my yarn, and made peace with my pen.
I admired the bare landscape and structure of nests.

Now preparations are upon us once more. As house painters, landscapers, and window washers are driving again.
The summer people are arriving; it is not yet summer.
They will travel by ferry, by plane, and with a little help from online – a car, or a boat, and a bicycle or two.

I don't see them yet, and still, I know they are coming.


The weather is only slightly warmer, but the sun is higher in the sky, and, thanks to daylight savings it's like heaven with sunlight that lasts 'til seven. You can't see them driving, biking, running, shopping, and parking everywhere; no, not yet.


The traffic is building, the streets are abuzz, the shops are still closed but the packages have come.
Though brown paper covers the windows, the unpacking is done – behind the doors, new merchandising is hung. The robins are dancing and the daffodils have sprung.


The sweet perfume of the lilac is here, and the peonies are popping.
The landscape is green, and with a smile, a nod and a wave -
I'll ride my bike or go for a hike. I'll look for birds on their wire, and the stars even higher. I will celebrate the moon in that grand month of June; the roads and sidewalks crowded again.

# Room Noise

**By Amy Jenness**

Water tinkles down
sighing pipes
Crow's wing clips
the frozen branch
Cat claws tick
on slippery teal
linoleum

The fridge motor kicks in

Clicking timekeepers
force march slender pointed
soldiers to the right,
to the right

The wind, constant
wind, sluices by
Sometimes a scream
but mostly a soft whisper

Something unseen
nestles down deeper
a beam, a brick
a tree leans in

## 6 OFF-SEASON

**By Harry Patz, Jr.**

The slow boat cut the engines, as the Brant Point lighthouse came into view on this sunny, but windy October afternoon. The fast ferry had passed them somewhere in the harbor some time ago. If Frank had taken it, he would have arrived an hour earlier. Not many people joined him on the slow boat; they were mostly day laborers of Cape employers who wouldn't pay the more expensive fees of the Hy-line. A few others were bringing their cars to the island. Not so for Frank. He didn't bring a car, and wasn't returning from work.

As the boat docked and sounded its horn, and eager folks grabbed their bags and packages to step into the crisp, clean air of Nantucket, all Frank could think to himself was: I hate this place.

Cars idled to pick up their friends and loved ones at the Steamship Authority Terminal, and some taxis joined them – the old standbys of Judy's Taxi, A-1 Taxi, and their compatriots in former cop cars and beat-up minivans. Shunning them, Frank grabbed his rollaway bag, a fading black veteran of many a Merrill Lynch junket, from the blue-tarped luggage return carts and began the short walk to the home on Hulbert Avenue. Well, at least it was a nice day. Yes, a nice day to begin my exile, he thought.

Passing the local fast food shops on Broad Street – chains like McDonald's were kept away by strict zoning, and Frank was thankful for that as well – he made the turn onto South Beach Street. He had walked here before, when the kids were young. Whenever they had gone into town, as of late, they usually had a driver. But most of their time wasn't spent in town. The restaurants, many of high quality, and some even beloved by well-heeled August visitors from New York and Boston, among other places, weren't good enough for his wife Victoria, or her family or her friends. They only sampled the exquisite cuisine of private chefs at whatever party, celebration, charity event, or cotillion was going on that Friday or Saturday night. And this among other reasons was why Victoria was becoming his ex-wife.

Frank made the right turn to Easton Street, and then passed the White Elephant hotel. If he had any fond memories of the many trips to Nantucket, they emanated from this area. When his children were young and unspoiled, he'd take them when Victoria was playing tennis, sleeping off her hangover, or "busy" with unnamed engagements on a Saturday morning, and they'd dig in the sand, ride the swings, or play wiffle ball on the lawn. This was when the kids still listened to him and looked at him as something other than a financier for whatever short-term monetary issue they had.

Frank happily remembered flying kites with them. Harris loved to send the kite high in the sky, and Mandy adored it when he would throw her to the heavens, then catch her descent into his arms. Those were the best times.

And Sunday mornings, at least occasionally if not every weekend, he could pull rank with Victoria, and get away from her family and friends. They'd have a nice breakfast at the White Elephant, sitting outside and enjoying Nantucket Harbor, just the four of them: Frank, Victoria, Harris and Mandy. It was Frank's favorite spot on the island. Victoria even pretended like she enjoyed it most times. But it didn't matter whether she did or didn't. What mattered to Frank was that he had his family together once a week, and his children were happy.

But that seemed ages ago. Harris had dropped out of Stanford a few years prior and was working at a tech start-up in the Bay Area. They didn't speak much, but Frank gathered the goal of his son's business was to "connect" busy men with girls outside of the male-dominated tech industry. Harris made it sound like he was changing the world but it felt more like a new version of Jim Lange and *The Dating Game*. Well, he hadn't asked for money…in the past three months.

Mandy was a junior at Vanderbilt. Her life seemed to revolve around sorority matters. Whenever Frank tried to have a discussion with Mandy about her academic performance, Victoria stepped in and pointed out Mandy's many "leadership" abilities in the sorority and the community in general. Mandy had come home at Christmas but departed after a few days to ski with her friends. She didn't return for any other break, and although she had stopped off at the house in Greenwich to switch out clothes in June, she spent the remainder of the summer between Nashville and her boyfriend's family's place in Virginia. All with her mother's approval.

Frank made the left onto Hulbert Avenue, and walked past the imposing homes. While their house was on the water in this highbrow neighborhood, it wasn't in the prime location of "the Cliffs," something that Victoria vowed to change "as God is my witness," as it was for Scarlett O'Hara in a different but altogether not too-dissimilar era. While being demoted to this allegedly pedestrian neighborhood, the house held a number of brilliant ocean views, including the second floor and the widow's walk.

Frank arrived and dropped his bag on the long, wraparound porch. The caretakers had removed the cushions from the chairs, but he thought he might have a drink and enjoy the waves among the high tide. He took out the keys and tried the lock. It didn't work. Taking a deep breath, he tried the key again. Did I have the right keys, he thought? Yes, the same, lighthouse key ring they'd had for ages. He tried each of the four keys on the ring, though he knew none of them would work. Frank then took out his Blackberry and made a call to the one person he didn't want to speak with. She picked up after five rings.

"Yes?"

"It's me. I just got here."

"Congratulations. What do you want?"

"The keys don't work. Is there a problem with the lock? Did Willie say anything when he cleaned out the pool?"

"The keys work perfectly fine…to the guesthouse. You didn't think you were actually going to stay in Daddy's house, did you?"

"You mean our house. That we, more accurately I, paid for all those years ago."

"And that we got for a song only because of Daddy's friend. Yes, I had the locks changed. The guesthouse is fine for your purposes. I'm sorry but while there is power, the cable and Internet won't be on until tomorrow. It just couldn't be helped."

"Unbelievable, Victoria."

"If you want to make a formal complaint, take it up with the lawyers," Victoria said as she hung up the line.

Frank carried his bag off the porch and headed to the guesthouse in the back, shaking his head. The key mercifully worked, and he looked at the functional, but Spartan dwelling: a tiny bedroom matched by a tiny living room (inoperable cable for today), and a galley kitchen with dishwasher and dinette (the name just conjured up TV dinners in the 1970s). A stackable washer and dryer were in one of the closets and provided a saving grace; Frank didn't bring many clothes. All told, less than 600 square feet. Victoria hadn't wanted to upgrade the guesthouse given that she believed a new "Tara" would come her way, and Frank had reluctantly agreed. Now, being unsure how long he would remain on Nantucket, he wished they had spruced it up. He opened up two windows to air out the musty smell.

Folding up the sailing blanket that was covering it, Frank plopped down on the couch, and put his feet up on the white, wooden coffee table.

Waking two hours later in darkness and the autumn chill, Frank lunged for the nautical-print blanket. Five minutes later, he opened his eyes again and checked his watch: 6:21 p.m. Rising to the bathroom, he combed his fading hair, and brushed his teeth. Staring at his pudgy, fifty-two year old countenance in the seashell-adorned mirror, he wondered to himself, how the hell did I get here? Ah, better not to think about.

With no food in the house – he planned to get groceries tomorrow – Frank looked at the evening's dinner plans as a Boy Scout might approach an exercise for a merit badge: the shortest distance between two points was a straight line. And that meant going to LoLa, the closest, open available restaurant. The place was always crowded in the summer, and from the outside, it looked like a New York City lounge with hip music blaring. Frank had heard the food was good, but it was another place on Victoria's verboten list. So location and spite were working to his advantage.

After a short walk, warmed by the lined Patagonia jacket Victoria had given him two Christmases ago, Frank walked into LoLa, and grabbed a seat at the bar, near the only other customer in the place, an older guy. Older was relative, Frank thought; the guy likely wasn't much more than sixty. Yet the short, cute, redheaded barmaid, with apparently a true name of Star, was definitely not a third of Frank's age, but wasn't quite half of it either. Placing a cocktail napkin down, she approached Frank.

"What can I get you?" Star asked pleasantly.

Frank cleared his throat. "Your menu says you have a Mandarin Mule. Can you also do the regular Moscow Mule? If so, which would you recommend?"

"Well, you can't go wrong with a classic."

"OK, the Moscow Mule it is."

"Are you also eating with us tonight?"

"Uh, yeah. Let's go with the burger and your four-cheese mac-and-cheese. My friend Nelson said it's good."

"Indeed it is. Thanks."

The white haired man two seats down from me at the bar leaned in. "Which Nelson is that?"

"Nelson Osgood," Frank responded. "He used to work with me at Merrill Lynch."

"Were you one of the 'Thundering Herd'?"

"I was, many moons ago. I'm out to pasture now," Frank added, laughing. Star placed the impossibly tall Moscow Mule in front of Frank. While it wasn't in the silver goblet cup, it looked impossibly delicious.

The gentleman probed a bit. "Was it the downturn, the M&A, or just your classic downsizing?"

"Probably all of the above. Throw in a little technological change, too. It is what it is. I'm figuring out what's next. Do you know Nelson?"

"We've met a few times, but I haven't seen him in a while. I'm Ernest. I own a few shops in the town."

"Frank Willoughby," he said as he extended his hand, "pleasure to meet you. What kind of shops do you run?"

"The usual T-shirt and sweatshirts, but we've branched out into sports gear, too. It's a living."

"Are you native to Nantucket?"

"I've been here twenty-seven years, but some people would still consider me a wash-ashore. I was in the banking world too, at Manny Hanny. But I got sick of keeping up with the Joneses. My wife didn't. She stayed in New York, and I came here. We're both better off."

Frank laughed a bit. "I'm going through a divorce myself. It's not exactly the same situation. I don't mean to pry Ernest, but how do you survive up here? Until today, I've never been up in Nantucket outside of the summer. It's pretty and all, but most people I've met in the past are assholes."

Ernest looked up at the ceiling for a few seconds and then returned his gaze back to Frank. "I'm sorry to hear about your divorce. But for me, and this was just my experience, it was a godsend. She got what she wanted and I got what I wanted. And I think Nantucket is one of the most beautiful places on earth. I did my fair share of traveling in my past life but still feel that way. As for the people, there are good ones and bad ones everywhere. You may just not have been looking in the right places when you have visited."

"I don't doubt you're right, Ernest. But doesn't it get desolate up here in the winter? I hear most things are closed until Christmas Stroll in December, and then after that it's a barren few months until late spring. Don't you go nuts?"

This time, Ernest didn't just lean in. He hopped to the adjacent stool next to Frank. "Let me let you in on a little secret…" pausing perhaps fifteen seconds for the full dramatic effect, "the offseason is the best time of the year. You'll see. Just don't tell the rest of them."

Frank smiled, and clinked glasses with Ernest, who then stood up. "I need to meet my girlfriend for dinner, so I'll be on my way." He left some money for Star on the bar, and then shook Frank's hand again. "Nice meeting you, Frank. I hope to see you around."

Frank turned to Star. "He seems like a real nice guy."

"The best," Star replied. "Your food should be coming right up."

Frank's track record for bargains with God hadn't worked so well the last few years, but after finishing the two Mules, the burger with seasoned fries, and the mac-and-cheese, he promised to God (and himself) he would exercise the next day. He knew the short walk home wouldn't count. But tomorrow, not just because of the coming cable TV and Internet, promised a new day.

The whirring sound of buzz saws awakened Frank a few shades after 8 a.m. It was not just a lone buzz saw; it seemed an army of them. Hordes of carpenters and workers apparently came from the procession of pick-up trucks and four-wheeled vehicles driving by the guesthouse. Frank had seen a number of homes being re-shingled yesterday, and the crews appeared to be getting an early start to maximize the mid-October sunlight.

Remembering his vow for exercise, Frank thought about taking a long walk, but he decided to really stretch himself. No, not a jog – that would be too adventurous for him – but a slow bike ride was the next intermediate step, even if he rode up and down Hulbert Avenue. With no food in the house, he would have to venture out for breakfast first. Star suggested that Fog Island Café had the best pancakes. Young's Bike Shop wasn't far from there, so the decision was made.

After securing *The Wall Street Journal* and the New York tabloids from The Hub, and with orange juice and coffee in front of him, he perused the Fog Island menu. The waitress confirmed the pancakes were outstanding, in a friendly, unobtrusive manner. Eschewing the classic buttermilk or even the blueberry offering, he nodded to the local surroundings and chose the cranberry pancakes. If not quite a local, it was a peace offering. Delighted with his choice, Frank left with two bags of Fog Island's own pancake batter for the guesthouse.

After renting a mountain bike at Young's Bicycle Shop, with a helmet that seemed less onerous than the one he used in the past, Frank decided on a short, southerly ride to Surfside Beach. The young man from the bike shop said it was a relatively flat ride, and at 7 miles round-trip, it would be a good way to "ease-into" his long-delayed returned to fitness.

Whenever they had arrived in Nantucket, often on Victoria's family's plane from Bridgeport, or occasionally Teterboro, New Jersey, Frank had suggested that the family take bike rides together. But any alleged exercise, even if it was for time with the kids, had to serve a social purpose. Thus, tennis or golf at the Club was Victoria's only approved activities.

Victoria, through her rigorous diet and her steady tennis game, preserved the impressive figure of her youth. Frank, unfortunately for him, had gone in the opposite direction. The weekly grind of late hours, client dinners, and corporate junkets left him round and bloated. Not quite halfway into the ride, he pulled off for a break. Stepping off the red bike, and taking a long, leisurely drink of his Gatorade, he looked at the building across Surfside road: The Muse.

The Muse, which also had a pizza sign, was a venue for bands and beer. The lack of windows was a dead giveaway that it must be a lively place. Frank had never visited, but on those many nights with Victoria that ended in a drag out fight, or even the ones petering out to a depressing, temporary truce, it was the kind of place he should have gone to clear his head. Nothing's stopping me now, he thought, and he made a mental note to visit on the weekend.

For the rest of the ride, and after his arrival to the barren Surfside parking lot, he thought of Victoria. These kinds of "public" beaches, with kids playing football and hot dog stands were repellent to her. Frank walked past the shuttered rest rooms and food stand down the path to the beach. Glad that he brought his Yale sweatshirt with him, as it was even windier close to the ocean on this sunny, fall day, he walked to the edge of the water. Sitting down, he watched with wonder as the powerful waves of the Atlantic Ocean bombarded the beach again and again.

When they met just after college, Victoria was Frank's muse. Beautifully blonde, with a well-shaped, tan body honed from years of tennis, how could he not fall in love with her? The differences between them didn't seem that great in those younger years, at least compared to any other girls he dated. But as they spent more time together, eventually marrying and then having children, the gaps seemed to widen just a bit more each year. Overlooked items or minor irritants explained away in great sex or resplendent, exotic vacations gave way to longer-term, simmering resentments. He could explain away the snobby nature of her family, as she didn't get to choose her family. And the way she treated people just outside her circle, with petty comments about their weight, how they really weren't good looking...well, this didn't matter as she was good to him, right?

The children happily came along after marriage. At first she was focused on them, and Frank understood, as he thought his primary function was to provide for them, despite the many inherent financial advantages from her family. Soon enough, though, the legion of help arrived to "make it easier" for her to connect with her friends and manage her "civic imperatives" in the community. Both Victoria and Frank became estranged from their kids, he at work and she with her commitments, and then increasingly from each other. And those minor irritants and overlooked items? Eventually the kids sadly adopted similar behaviors as well.

Frank co-existed for a long-time, doing his best to soldier onward. The success at work buoyed him, even if he didn't recognize his wife as much, while the sweet memories of his young children morphed into the reality of distant, moody, and self-absorbed young adults. He had a front-row seat for much of the drama, during the weekends and extended summer vacations in resplendent Nantucket. The workweek in New York and their lonely home in Greenwich both became oases of calm during each increasingly petulant summer. The years went by swiftly, as Frank continually isolated himself from the calendar and reality.

Frank shivered beneath his heavy, fully-zipped sweatshirt. The delayed return-trip back to Hulbert Avenue ultimately won its battle with the continuous jabbing wind at Surfside, and Frank made his way back to the bike. Taking just a slight detour in the streets adjacent to the beach, he took a quick spin by the empty youth hostel. Turning the bicycle onto Surfside road, he headed back to town.

Frank returned to town without stopping. He was proud of himself, though not many others would be, for completing a ride of roughly seven total miles. After picking up takeout provisions at Stubby's on Broad Street (grilled-chicken Panini, baked potato chips and a diet Coke), he biked back to the guesthouse. The cable man had visited and left him with the crucial lifelines to TV and the Internet, but it didn't seem all that urgent for him to get online.

Sufficiently warmer than the beach, and smelling crisp autumnal air amid the competing buzz saws, Frank ate his lunch facing the water. Even with all the construction activity, the serenity of the harbor relaxed him and gave him a moment's peace. Despite prior plans for the needed food shopping, Frank went inside and lay down for a nap.

Frank awoke surprisingly refreshed and invigorated a few hours later. The sea air and his strenuous bike ride had given him the best sleep since he knew his union with Victoria was truly over. He could argue with himself about any number of specific moments when the bridge between them collapsed. But he understood it was a slow gradual process. The events of the past few months, finally being let go from Bank of America, the vestigial owner of his beloved Merrill Lynch, and the realization that Mandy wouldn't be spending school breaks at home any longer, left Victoria with no more pretenses to keep. Her affairs with the downtown artist and the lawyer from Darien were almost beside the point. She wanted out.

And so that is how Frank arrived in Nantucket, his own Napoleonic exile to Elba. It was the last place he wanted to go but the easiest place to keep a fractured peace. Not dealing with her had not been the best long-term relationship strategy but it had helped him survive. And thus would he employ it again.

She could have the friends and cocktails of her crowd in Connecticut, with all the phony acolytes who would tell her how aggrieved she was while repeatedly reinforcing what a loser her husband turned out to be. He could escape and plot his next move, and not live in a sterile condo or re-purposed corporate housing. As Nelson had told him, "if you're going to be paying for two homes, you might as well live in one of them."

And in the throes of his depression, on that Thursday afternoon, after his bike ride, seeing stellar views of the Atlantic and a lunch outside, and strengthened by a restful nap, he felt a slight improvement in his mood. In booting up his computer and getting on-line, he expected to find that magical email with a new job, or Linked-In connection that would change his fate. While his non-alcoholic buzz wasn't completely killed, his only communications were from attorneys and junk email for Cialis and Viagra.

A short while later, Frank tried another place within walking distance for dinner: The Brotherhood of Thieves. The Brotherhood was one of those pubs he had seen in town, but due to their countless commitments and outright ban from Victoria, he had never visited. The sign on the door reminded him of some of the cartoon meanies in the Beatles' *Yellow Submarine* movie.

After entering through the heavy wooden door, Frank smiled at the décor of the place. With dark lighting, and heavily accented with wood and brick, its low ceilings made him believe the pub dated back to the Revolution. Though he knew this was not the case, he loved it just the same. Saddling up to the bar, he quickly ordered an Allagash White, brewed from Maine. On this cold, nippy night, where he had seen his breath on the walk into town, the thought of a steaming French Onion soup lured him more than a St. Bernard with brandy to an injured skier. Finally, he ordered a classic BroHo burger, along with curly fries.

The bar was still relatively quiet at 6 p.m. A younger couple in their late 20s was sitting down the other side of the bar, four stools away. They welcomed him into their conversation.

"Hi, I'm Jessica, and this is my husband Albert."

"Good evening. Frank Willoughby. Pleasure to meet you. Are you guys locals?"

"Yes we are," said Jessica. "Well, sort of. I moved here to take a teaching job last summer. Albert joined me. We're from Rhode Island."

"By way of New York, at least for me," Albert interjected. "I worked for Cantor Fitzgerald a few years out of college. But I hated it. I guess we're starting over in Nantucket. I'm doing some carpentry, some real estate, a little of everything."

"Well, how do you like it so far?" Frank asked.

"I love it. It's been everything we thought. Beats the hell out of the pace and nonsense of New York. The people are great," Albert added.

"I'd have to agree, though we've been warned the winters are tough, particularly in January and February. But I guess we'll see," Jessica added. "I take it you are a visitor, Frank?"

Frank paused for a minute, unsure of how best to answer. "We've had a house for years and came up often during the summer. But now, I have some downtime, so I am seeing it in the offseason." Frank paused another moment. "Truthfully...I'm getting divorced."

"I'm sorry to hear that Frank," Jessica responded, "and I hope it works out the way you want it. Hopefully you can explore the island a bit."

"I'm starting to. It's amazing how much I missed when I was busy the past few summers doing other things. I went on a bike ride today, which was great. Hopefully I can do more tomorrow, as the weather looks good all week. But I need to get some groceries."

Albert piped in. "You should try Bartlett Farm. You can ride your bike there, or drive. They have great fresh produce, pre-made meals, and some other interesting items. Cisco Brewery is right next door, in case you want to stock up there. We love it!"

"After a sales pitch like that, how could I say no?" Frank laughed as he also signaled Mike the bartender. "How about another Allagash for me, and a round for my new friends over there?"

After finishing his French Onion soup, and the burger, Frank parted ways from the young couple and walked home. The first two days haven't been so bad, he thought. He wondered if he should call home and check-in. Not that his call would be needed or wanted, but for him it just felt like the thing to do.

Arriving home after a circuitous walk on Main Street, which was mostly deserted despite the town's many signs displayed in the store windows to "Keep Downtown Thriving," he reluctantly grabbed up his Blackberry and called Victoria at the house. She picked up, and answered in a clinical voice above the din in the background.

"What do you need? Did the cable men come?" she asked tersely.

"Yes, no problem there."

"Well, what is it then?"

"I just…wanted to see how you're doing."

"I'm fine. I have guests here. The Wilsons are over for cocktails. And a few others."

"The Wilsons never miss a free drink."

"Spare me, Frank. You have a good night." He could almost hear her exasperated, mocking sigh to the others as she hung up the phone.

Frank gave a sigh of his own, albeit a different one, and turned on the TV. Flipping through the channels, he came upon a local Nantucket civic meeting. They were debating the zoning issue for a new chain supermarket. His other options at that hour included reruns of yet-another "Housewives" show and the tired *Wheel of Fortune*. The debate was surprisingly interesting, and he was impressed how one of the local selectmen, Callie Potter, passionately defended the need to preserve the town's character.

Frank awoke the next morning, and secured a bike rack and saddlebag from Young's after breakfast. He then set out for Bartlett's farm for his long-delayed shopping. The ride would be the same length as the one to Surfside, but the bike fellow warned him that the route wasn't as flat. Today is the first day of the rest of my life, he thought to himself.

Frank arrived at the farm without stopping once on the three-mile ride. Expecting the equivalent of a glorified roadside stand selling fresh produce, he was surprised that it was a full functioning farm, with real animals and fields, and something akin to a mini-supermarket, with wonderfully fresh produce.

Conscious of the limits of what he could transport back, Frank gathered cold cuts, items for salad (that first day thing again), and some beverages. But he did allow himself to look at the freshly prepared meals, where the Jamaican jerk chicken was tantalizing him.

When the server finished preparing his container, the customer behind him began to order. Frank saw that it was Callie, the selectman from the night prior, ordering pasta salad. Callie was an attractive woman in her mid 40s. Frank noticed she was not wearing a ring.

After she finished placing the order, Frank approached her. "Are you Callie Potter? I saw you last night on TV at the meeting."

"Yes I am! But that was taped a few days ago. Are you one of my constituents?"

"Sort of. I'm Frank Willoughby. We, I mean I have a summer place, but I am having an extended stay in the fall. So I'm trying to see some of the places I normally didn't get to."

"Well, this is definitely near the top of the list. They have everything, and most of the food is grown locally. I used to pick the strawberries with my kids when they were very little. But that was ages ago."

"Wow, sounds great. I wish I did that when my kids were young. We were too busy…with other stuff. Now they're grown and onto the next thing. I guess I am too…I'm finalizing my divorce."

"I'm sorry to hear that Frank. I lost my husband three years ago. My kids are grown and off-island, too. But there's plenty to do here. That's why I ran for selectman. It keeps me busy, and I love Nantucket deeply." Callie looked at her watch. "Well, it was nice meeting you Frank. I hope you have fun exploring the island."

The server handed Callie the chicken, and she walked to the checkout stand. He then turned to Frank, next in line. "Are you finding everything you need here, sir?"

Frank stood for a minute watching Callie cross the store, her hair swinging, and jeans smoothly fitting her hips, as the sun shone through the glass doors beyond checkout.

"I believe I am, Jeff," Frank responded to his own wonderment, "So much more than I expected."

## 7. TO BE A BEGGAR

**By Ursula Austin**

At that time my mother had left my father to find a job. She was very tired of his simply scratching out a living with a minimum of bare essentials. She loved him deeply but this was no life, this vegetating state. He of course was justified. He had been incarcerated in an enemy labor camp during World War II and came out, practically a skeleton when he reunited with us.

Life on the farm had been interesting but there was scant money and almost no food outside of what one could forage. It was this that drove her into the city and by a miracle, she found a childhood friend on the street car, who offered her a job.

When money arrived for us from her paycheck, my father was so mortified that he vowed to find a better job and "truly" support us. He too left for the city and it was just Gran and me for a while when suddenly everything changed. Father had indeed found a job. He was working for the United Nations Resettlement Agency and whom were they resettling? All the paperless, orphaned, displaced refugees of all ages all backgrounds, in other words DPS or simply Displaced Persons who now lived in DP settlements.

Father was posted to various settlements helping to process DP emigration. There were many rules and qualifications. The handicapped were ineligible for emigration, as were those who tested positive for TB. For the latter a skin test was the deciding factor. Sometimes there was heart break like with the Ukrainian Orthodox Priest, married with five beautiful daughters. One of the daughters tested positive for TB, so she could not emigrate but the rest of the family could. The priest and his wife chose to stay together rather than break up the family. They considered themselves lucky to have come out of World War II intact.

Then too there was Afanasi, the remarkable dark haired youth with the most melting brown eyes. He had seen his sister and mother killed when a grenade hit their country cottage. He heard the screams. He lost his arm rushing into the burning house trying to save them. Now he was with a wooden arm and ineligible to emigrate. I remember how he would come to visit us and my father had tried so hard to petition the Emigration Committee to at least let him go to a non-descriptive country, with fewer restrictions, like Australia or Uruguay. But the applications always came back stamped "rejected." Afanasi grew sadder, a sort of tristesse appeared in his eyes and my childish love for him grew stronger and stronger until one day he did not come and I heard whispers that he had died.

As each experience unfolded itself, one learned lessons of attachment and loss in these settlements.

Perhaps the strangest posting was on the edge of a picturesque town with a medieval castle. This settlement turned out to be unique. Here I have to offer a little background. In each of the settlements there were solid friendships formed as there were choice playmates. I never wanted for games or companions. But in this last settlement with the distant castle, I could not find any children to play with, let alone children at all. For days I walked around the settlement lonely, alone in thought, speculating on what had happened to all my past companions. Surely not every single one of them had emigrated.

Of course this was a new posting and perhaps if I explored enough, I would come across children somewhere. After all it was summer and school was out children had to be somewhere. This settlement was a little more official looking than the others. Here we had a gate and sentries in army uniforms—how strange. You could not go out the gates by yourself, there had to be an adult with you. I had a sense of imprisonment. In the eastern side of the settlement there was a large excavation and daily I heard bulldozers and other large machines until one sunny day—how well I remember that day—a cornflower blue sky, clear warm sunshine, silence no more machines. In place of bulldozing sounds I heard laughter not just any laughter but joyous, pealing laughter—I wanted to find the source. The excavation was now surrounded by bushes and there was a four square, comfortable looking building nearby. As I got closer to the excavation and the source of the laughter, I felt my heart beating faster and faster with anticipation. At last I found an opening in the bushes and as I went past it there was a swimming pool with lots of smiling heads bobbing—but with one difference. These were bodies with some missing an arm or a leg. They were in the pool swimming, playing water polo. I was bewildered until an adult approached me, greeted me and explained this settlement was a permanent home for all the wounded survivors (of the war) and since they are automatically disqualified from emigration they will live here—near this medieval castle. I watched a little longer and then felt self conscious, guilty because I had every limb on my body. I had not suffered as these people must have. Thoughts of sadness filled me, as I ran home to supper.

The next day was an anti-climax but I stayed away from the pool. I thought it was rude to be a gawker. So I wandered the periphery of the camp, dragging my feet in the dirt—slowly wandering when I heard a child's voice.

"Hey, hey who are you?"

I turned around and there stood a freckle faced, snub nosed little girl, seemingly spunky except that she had one crutch under an arm and was missing a leg.

"Do you want to play?" she continued.

"Yes, I do."

And she whisked me off to a series of small houses and there suddenly in front of my eyes was a cluster of maimed children. I wondered if their parents had been in the pool? But it was later explained to me—later after introductions that these children were orphans and they lived in these little houses, in clutches. I was taken into one of the houses and there were tables, single beds all looked like they had been built by Lilliputians. The children had been allowed to build their own furniture and had been given tools and wood. There were little kitchens with working ovens and each house had an assigned cook that would come and prepare meals for the children. There were weekly visits from nurses, doctors. There was a school that was being built to be ready in the fall. The children themselves had hordes of chewing gum, chocolate bars and tons of comics. They bestowed me with some gum, candy telling me they had an endless supply line for these things. As time went by I also learned that they acquired certain luxury items for their cooks by bartering various items on the black market. Their resilience and cleverness astounded me.

After a few weeks the children took me into their confidence. They explained that the sentries at the gate changed weekly and the children would simply send the most vulnerable looking, disabled set of children five or six out to the new sentries, to beg. As the children stood there looking forlorn, the sentries would ply them with gum, candy, comics sometimes crayons and pencils. The comics and the chocolate bars fetched the most on the black market and these were what the children aimed at preferably.

Soon they explained it was time to train me as a beggar. With my fair looks, I might be able to get them some extra goods. We went outside to a remote section of the settlement. I was nervous and excited. Would I pass muster, I wondered? The lesson began.

"Well you are not missing an arm or a leg so this will be hard," began Annie my coach.

She lined five chosen candidates out of the eighteen attendees.

"First," she said, "can you look sad like this."

She had one little boy with a missing arm demonstrate and then a girl with just a stump and a crutch demonstrate a higher level of sadness—despair. I wasn't sure how to do this. I tried at first but I kept wrinkling up my face so the children merely laughed and instructed me to differentiate between comical and sadness. Comical was a lost cause but soulful sadness was rewarded! I kept trying and trying until at last my eyes seemed to communicate the needed quality. Then one of the maimed boys spoke up.

"She'll need to have snot running down her nose and if she can contrive a limp, we'd be all set."

I was completely flummoxed. Forcing snot to run down one's nose was very difficult when one didn't have a cold. One of the children hobbled into one of the houses and after a while returned with handkerchief full of chopped onion. He told to hold it to my nose and not only did the snot run but a flood of tears as well.

"That's good," said Annie my coach.

Examining me she exclaimed, "You'll need to turn your feet in and do not look the sentries in the eye, just look down on the ground. Try to be really sad and rumple your clothes ahead of time, so you look disheveled as well."

All these elements were difficult to accomplish. I practiced with the children for several hours until I had won their approval.

"We will have another practice session tomorrow and then the next day you will go begging with us," my coach declared.

I went home exhausted that afternoon. I slept so well, ate a hearty breakfast the next morning.

I couldn't wait for my next adventure with the children. So it was once again, I made my way to the small houses and found my teacher Annie. We began our sessions immediately. This time a very small piece of onion in the handkerchief and a distinct limp on my part won instant approval.

"Oh yes, you are ready," said my teacher and her assistants.

We played interesting games, the rest of the afternoon. The children had invented games that required no tree climbing. They began with old fashioned hide-and-seek and then it was 'hide the tiger' to simple I spy games and eventually guessing games, finalized with predicting what the sentries would "give" them, how much I would bring into the pot?

At last the day to approach the sentries came. I was very nervous but Annie had been so specific where and how to stand, I felt reassured. We got to the gate. The children stood in a row. I wasn't in line yet, this was deliberate, it took me longer to get there with my limp. Such clever calculation! The children had their hands outstretched, those who had arms and hands. Those who didn't, stood like statues with their eyes cast down. At last I joined the line-up, with my rumpled clothes, snot running down my nose and looking down, feet turned in. I thought I was pathetic enough!

The sentries said something patted some of us on the head. They went into their little guard hut and came out with the goods: packs of gum for everyone, chocolates for some of us and comic books for all, as an afterthought there were small packets of M&M's for us, and boxes of crayons. We had loot. This was a "good haul," according to our leader. We headed back to the houses. I was officially declared a minimally useful beggar. My share automatically went to their households as I certainly didn't need it.

My life continued to revolve around my beggar clan, until my father's post was terminated and there was a new settlement to be transferred to. I was very sad to have to leave my friends. But they in true bravura said we must have a farewell party. The day before we were to leave the settlement, I went to Annie's house by invitation. The house looked festive, there were paper garlands, strange flowers and weeds in a nicked vase. There was food, a sausage and potato dish, and of course chocolate for desert.

Someone had placed a small pink box on one of the beds. After the feast and playing our usual round of games we came back inside—I was given a few, select classic comics and then the pink box was presented. At their urging I opened it and inside was silver locket which opened up. On one side of the locket were etched the words, " To be," and on the other side of the locket, " a beggar."

Naturally I was overwhelmed by this gift and wept real tears without an onion in a hankie. I put it on. Annie helped fasten the clasp around my neck as all the children surrounded me and shouted, "Now you'll never forget us." And indeed I haven't.

## Nantucket Haiku

### by Ursula Austin

daffodils push forth
despite blizzard's frosty snow
soon spring's sunny glow

## Wanting to Soar

### by Ursula Austin

fallow fields in other places
full moons
deer tracks
other traces
lifting the day
into Orion's belt
heart beating
catching breath
wanting to soar
avian ways distanced
all the more.
One cannot tame
those creatures
nor could their
emblazoned hue
be described
they tincture nature
just to survive

## 7. COFFEE

**By K. Miller**

Breakfast was a serious meal just like dinner. School days and weekends were the same when mother and father were in town. Miss Rosa set the sunroom table with a white linen tablecloth that grandfather had woven in Scotland before he moved to Nantucket. We had to be very careful never to get any spills on it. The white plates were set out, never the bone china, two glasses at each place setting, one for milk the other for juice and the stainless cutlery in the morning as the  sterling was reserved for dinner. Fresh flowers were always placed in front of fathers seat so that he would notice. Each morning, he would sit down and say, "Dear these are for you" as he slid the vase across the table to set in front of mother's place. Her mother lived with us in a separate apartment but she was never invited for breakfast or dinner yet we used her linens and dishes. Although Nana's apartment was attached to our home, mother said, "Your grandmother has her own home and routine and she needs her privacy."

Father liked having half of a pink grapefruit with sugar as his first course with the sections precut, which was usually my job. There was a special grapefruit spoon placed to the right of the coffee spoon at each place setting that had a serrated edge and if you weren't very careful it would cut your mouth as well as the grapefruit.

If the phone rang during a meal no one was allowed to answer, the caller was told the family is taking their meal, please leave a message and they will ring you back. Father was the exception, Mother said, "Your father is someone very important and people need to speak with him right away. When he takes a call everyone must stop talking and be very quiet" When father was talking we weren't eating either, he could talk a very long time. When he was at the table he rarely said a word so we ate quickly and asked to be excused. I looked forward to school letting out because I was usually invited for tea with Nana in the afternoons. I chattered away with stories about my day and questions about hers, I watched her knit and she watched me draw until Mother fetched me away to help prepare dinner.

The menus were posted in the kitchen each week and breakfast was the only meal that never changed except by the day of the week. Pancakes and waffles were only served on Saturday's. I didn't like Monday's because it was back to school and it was pork chop day. Miss Rosa and her husband would kill a pig now and then for the chops and bacon and save the tenderloins for Nana to cook. I didn't like seeing any of the animals killed that we ate: squirrel, alligator, rattlesnake, possum, rabbits and turtles. I ate the fish and shrimp and never liked the meat. Miss Rosa would cut the pork chops real thin and cook them up on a grill outside. She made grits, oven biscuits, cream gravy and fried eggs.

Coffee was served to mother and father after the first course was taken away. Father drank his with a squirt of artificial sweetener; mother took two lumps of sugar and some cream. After thoroughly mixing the ingredients in her coffee, she would take her toast or biscuit dip it in the coffee and say, "Now children, this is considered rude, never do this out in public" as she double dunked and then bit off the coffee soaked part. When I turned 16, mother said that I was a young lady and old enough for some coffee now and then. She offered me some of the pre-dipped biscuit she had been eating. I respectfully declined because I didn't eat off other people's plates as she had taught me this was rude as well.

Several years later, Nana and I took a little trip to Nantucket for a break from our family and for her to remember being a young bride there. One morning we had breakfast at a wonderful restaurant and ordered eggs and donuts and coffee. The waitress asked if I took cream and sugar and I said,

"Yes mame." As we stirred our cups to dissolve the sugar, without a word of planning, we both picked up our donuts and dunked them in the coffee and took a bit of the coffee soaked part. Whenever I smell coffee, I think of eating soggy biscuits and other things we do when no one is looking.

## Brief Respite

### By Julianne Kever

Off the worn path,
flash of fluttering red invites me.
Past poison ivy and decaying bark
I make my way to visit.

Stepping over black trumpets and Indian pipes
that seem to bow out of my way,
I admire up close the young tree that brought me.

I'd like to settle on nearby moss
to nap awhile, wake, see it all there
painted just for me, private gallery
of grasses, green and trees.

Yet, I hear others coming near;
my brief respite broken, I say my thanks,
head to see what next may lure me away.

# 8. FROM NANTUCKET TO MARS

By Paula Korn

### Prologue

*Since people began living on Earth they have ventured out to explore the unknown – in search of food, water, shelter, knowledge, challenge, property and economic gain. In 1969, two Americans took the first steps on the Moon. In the 21st Century, people from Earth now look beyond the moon – to Mars.*

### The First Landing, 2030

The first crewed landing on Mars in 2030 carried four NASA astronauts with extensive experience in spaceflight. It was a successful mission, but not without its moments of critical urgency – both in flight and on the Martian surface. Following that historic mission, NASA's plan called for a crewed mission every six years, beginning in 2040, supported by interval cargo missions that would bring water, oxygen, food and material supplies.

Those first astronauts arrived on the planet with enough supplies for two years, which would last until the next Earth-Mars alignment for return to Earth. After an eight-month journey to the Red Planet, the small team used the tools they brought to burrow deep into the Martian regolith to install radiation-protected living quarters below the planet's surface. They brought various types of packaged and frozen food and eventually tested out a new aquaculture process that would yield an adequate amount of fresh vegetables. They had a six-month supply of air and water, which would be rationed until their environmental closed loop systems could be constructed, tested and put into service.

The four pioneers established a base that would support future missions, including an environmental protection system, communications post, robotics station, science center, fitness facility and storage units for food and supplies. They explored their surroundings, taking brief hikes on the surface and extended buggy excursions to collect rocks, search for water and document various phenomena. They observed the Martian skies, the windstorms and atmospheric changes, and kept individual daily journals recording scientific, psychological and physiological notations as well as general impressions of their experiences.

While they were responsible for carrying out a lengthy schedule of procedures and experiments, and a full regimen of daily exercise, the astronauts' schedule was programmed much the same as time spent aboard the International Space Station for about 20 years. But the station had traveled in an orbit that averaged 240 miles above the Earth and most crews spent no longer than a few weeks or months per visit. Communications with NASA occurred in real-time, throughout the day.

Living on Mars was different.

It took nearly eight months to travel the 35-million miles between Earth and Mars, when the planets were closely aligned, as they traveled along their orbits around the sun. After a period of two years on Mars, the return trip to Earth could be initiated with the next planetary alignment. Visiting Mars was far more challenging than those one-day trips to the Space Station.

There was a 40-minute delay in the communications link between Earth and Mars. NASA initiated three scheduled transmissions a day with reports and updates. The astronauts would respond to each transmission. But they were basically on their own, communicating with each other while problem solving in real time – it was a far more independent experience than for any previous astronaut mission. In the event of an urgent matter, the four could communicate with Earth at any time but, due to the time delay, they could depend on an immediate reply taking an hour and a half. Learning to be resourceful was the key to adjusting to life on Mars.

When the astronauts returned to Earth, the Americans celebrated with parades across the nation, visits with school children and presentations throughout the world. The United States had, yet again, demonstrated their leadership in space – but not for long.

While plans were now in development for the first Mars colony, mission objectives grew murky. The U.S. had met the ultimate challenge. Those who had read about the first missions to the moon, a hundred years earlier, were taunted by the quirky familiarity of U.S. leadership in space. Americans landed on the moon and then abandoned the program after a handful of missions, having won "the space race" with the Soviet Union in the 1960s. Would they abandon Mars as well?

Several nations were now focused on space endeavors of their own, on orbit around Earth and around the Moon, in space stations of various sizes and shapes, as well as a variety of objectives. Among their accomplishments were materials and life sciences developments, robotic systems, mining sorties on the lunar surface and, ultimately, significant profit-making scenarios.

## Mars Colony One, 2050

The first U.S. mission to establish a colony on Mars arrived in 2050, years beyond the originally projected schedule. Lack of public commitment, compromised budgets, political erosion and technology setbacks had threatened nearly every effort. NASA had reorganized into a public/private organization for space exploration and economic development, transitioning much of the logistics and operations to commercial partners and contractors. But, as a result of the instability in government funding, only two cargo spacecraft carrying supplies for the Mars colony were sent during the first ten years. Members of the colony scrambled to survive.

All but two people did survive that first decade on Mars. One had suffered significant physical problems during the flight from Earth and died shortly after the landing – the other succumbed to radiation poisoning due to an early technical failure in the environmental control and life support system. Life on Mars had become an extraordinary feat of navigating one threatening challenge after another, all linked with magical solutions and well-earned discoveries.

The colonists expanded and improved living quarters with new infrastructure and composite materials. They had studied and evaluated the extensive reports of the four astronauts who established and lived at the first Mars base camp, 2030-2032. There were many lessons learned. From that first experience, together with advancing science and technology, the colonists were more informed and confident. They organized themselves in teams based on expertise and revamped the base camp to accommodate more people and activities. They had specific goals and objectives scheduled throughout their 10-year program.

It wasn't until the delay of the first cargo mission that concern crept into the group consciousness. Only six months before the cargo was due to arrive, NASA informed the colony that the mission would be delayed for two years. The successful, confident colonists responded with anger, dismay and fear.

And then the work began. They focused on immediate issues and requirements: food, water and air. They became more resourceful and creative – problem solving at every turn. Survival became the motivating priority that unified and energized the 18 Americans of Mars Colony One.

On Earth, the U.S. was continuing on a path of developing nascent technologies to support the Mars missions. In collaboration with the National Network for Manufacturing Innovation, engineers were advancing technological innovations for American manufacturers while supporting the exploration of Mars. But recent developments in technology were gaining a more urgent objective for creating a permanent settlement on Mars – global climate changes were escalating.

As far back as 2014, the U.N. Intergovernmental Panel on Climate Change (IPCC) was urging all nations to cooperate in addressing and mitigating the increasing risks of climate change. The panel advocated for collaboration in managing risks and uncertainties through informed climate policy, and for the implementation of economic development and adaptation that would proceed in a sustainable manner, ensuring food production would not be threatened.

Economic and population growth – both energy-consuming concepts – were the most significant drivers in the increases in carbon emissions from fossil fuel combustion. The IPCC report addressed both risks and opportunities for societies, economies and ecosystems around the world. While studies and data collection proliferated in nearly all of the developed nations, and world leaders were calling for action, the concept of taking responsibility for sustainability did not attain adequate traction on a large scale.

In 2015, the U.S. and the French collaborated on a remote sensing satellite system to conduct the first global survey of Earth's surface water and map ocean surface height with unprecedented detail. The implementation of the Surface Water and Ocean Topography mission helped to develop new approaches to observe and understand the changing climate and water resources. The resulting data was intended to support decision makers in their analysis of how to anticipate and act to influence events that impacted people on Earth.

With global change exacerbating environmental conditions on Earth – the warming temperatures of air and water, erratic atmospheric events, rising oceans, draughts and floods, carbon intensification in the atmosphere – more nations were becoming involved in Mars programs that focused on access and colonization. Many considered the initiation of the international team on Mars Colony Two as a necessity.

**The Landing of Mars Colony Two, 2060**

In 2060, the now ten-year-old Mars Colony One was anticipating the long-awaited arrival of the first visitors from Earth. The event was marked with excitement, stirred by an edgy mix of uncertainties.

Would the newcomers fit into the now established American community? Would they understand the risks and unknowns of the Mars environment? The new colonists, an international group representing diverse experience and expertise, would bring their own uncertainties.

The last communications transmission from Earth indicated the incoming spacecraft of new colonists was due to arrive shortly. By now, the spacecraft would be separated from its orbiting support vehicle and beginning to descend through the thin Martian atmosphere. The communications officer at the new Mars relay station does her best to make contact with the spacecraft, but the transmission is fragmented at best – an incoming vehicle has never before attempted contact with an outpost on Mars. It is, after all, the first time humans would welcome other humans on a foreign planet.

The observation officer makes an initial sighting of the incoming spacecraft, as it descends to the surface. It looks promising, but heading several miles off target. He gives orders to the on-surface transportation team to ready all three transport rovers, as well as the old buggy from the 2030 mission, which they had rehabilitated only a couple of years ago. The team also prepares the colony's two hovercraft to transport incoming supplies, baggage and, hopefully, the requested Makerbot Replicators.

The new residents will use the latest edition of these 3D printers to fabricate additional, upgraded housing, rovers, an air and water processing center, a new aquaculture lab, additional advanced infrastructure, and other innovations the new International Space Agency and its commercial partners have organized to make life on Mars more efficient, safe and environmentally accommodating.

Ten of the original 20 colonists will remain on the planet, serving as the "elders" of the community. Eight have opted to return to Earth. Some will join the Mars planning team for further mission development, some will retire from NASA and join one of the thriving new commercial exploration companies, some will address physical and emotional issues that could not be resolved on Mars – it's not, apparently, for everyone. After ten years, the incoming spacecraft presents the first opportunity to make the long voyage home.

Transporting the people, equipment and supplies from the remote landing site, more than ten miles away, will take a few hours. It's yet another first for Colony One. Each of the two cargo missions had arrived close to the established landing site and did not include people, let alone those about to egress from a six-month long journey. At least the new interspace solar electric powered propulsion system was able to shorten the transit time from Earth.

The International Space Station, which orbited the Earth until 2024, was used as a test bed for demonstrating many of the new technologies in the microgravity environment of space, achieving research breakthroughs not possible on Earth. The orbiting laboratory also advanced understanding of how the body changes in space over time and how to protect astronaut health for the longer duration missions of the future.

NASA's Human Research Program and the National Space Biomedical Research Institute had initiated a research and technology program on astronaut health and performance for these exploration missions. The known challenges of traveling to and living on Mars included the impact of the space environment on various aspects of human health, such as visual impairment, behavioral health, bone loss, cardiovascular alterations, human factors and performance, neurobehavioral and psychosocial factors and sensorimotor adaptation.

The development and application of smart medical systems and technology continued to be a priority. Mission planners and system developers had learned earlier to monitor and mitigate human risks and develop countermeasures for problems experienced during long-duration space travel. Now, their objective has evolved toward preparing for a permanent settlement on Mars.

Landing safely on a previously unexplored area of the Mars surface, members of the newly arrived international team cross the barren Red Planet on the transport rovers. They bring a newly charged agenda to generate new approaches for sustainability and adaptation. Mars Colony Two will embark on this next articulated objective, based on the success of the newly revitalized and independently sustained community of Nantucket Island.

## Nantucket Island, Massachusetts, 1660-2060

Nantucket, the "far away island" 30 miles at sea, off the coast of New England, had a long history of independence and innovation. The 14-mile island was what remained of an ancient receding glacier. When the English began to settle on the island in the 1660s, they learned lessons of endurance from the Native Americans who had inhabited the little island for several hundred years, sustaining their tribes by fishing, hunting and farming.

In the early 1700s, with recent developments in the processing and applications of spermaceti oil, islanders explored the potential of harvesting the precious resource and in 1712 the community set off on what was to become the world's first international export business.

Whaling was the fundamental impetus for the growth and prosperity of Nantucket, which became the whaling capital of the world by the 1750s. Oil from sperm whales evolved as the source of light for the dark nights on the island and throughout much of the developed world.

But the substantial wealth and growth of the island was not to continue. By the mid-1800s, the harbor became impassable for the large whaling vessels, the Civil War brought many of the whalers to the battlefield, the California Gold Rush became a mecca for wealth development, electric light was growing popular in homes, shops and offices, and petroleum was being explored for energy applications.

Nantucket Town, with its magnificent mansions, banking institutions and economic success, grew no more. But while the town became an architectural time capsule, much of the island was enjoying an agricultural renaissance, with more than a hundred farms in operation by 1875.

Industrialization at the end of the 19th Century began to attract some wealthy summer visitors to the island in search of escape from the bustling cities to the clean sea air. Artists also trickled to the island and, by the 1920s the beginnings of an art colony began to take shape. But economic depression and war took a toll.

Noting the town's three centuries of historical documentation, structures and charm, Walter Beinecke, an energetic and creative developer, took interest in Nantucket in the 1960s. He restored and rebranded Nantucket as a destination for wealthy visitors. In 1972, the U.S. Government recognized the revitalized island as a National Historic Landmark. A rejuvenated artist colony emerged and played a significant role in the fabric of the community.

By the end of the 20th Century, the Chamber of Commerce was transforming the once sleepy island into a popular vacation resort community with a burst of businesses, festivals and tourist events, set against a vintage backdrop of historic cobblestone roads, buildings, churches and a whaling museum.

In 2015, Nantucket engaged in a program to develop more capable energy technologies in order to accommodate its flourishing economy. The town submitted a proposal to NASA for an advanced energy storage system that would serve to provide energy for the island with a more efficient, sustainable approach as well as lower costs.

NASA's solicitation for proposals featured two category areas: "High Specific Energy System Level Concepts," focused on cell chemistry and system-level battery technologies, such as packaging and cell integration, and "Very High Specific Energy Devices," focused on energy storage technologies beyond the current theoretical limits of Lithium batteries, while maintaining the cycle life and safety characteristics demanded of energy storage systems used in space applications.

NASA funded Nantucket's proposal because it addressed both of these areas with innovative and creative approaches. Power for the community would use an adaptation of flow potential gradient (FPG). Although the FPG effect was known in laboratories as early as 1998, the island became the site of the first commercial application of what would be regarded as the energy breakthrough of the 21st Century. Nantucket's Independent Colony Model program was gaining momentum.

Initial tests on Nantucket revealed it to be a "floating" voltaic cell. The island quickly established its own energy capabilities. As a result of this accomplishment, the island was able to become energy sufficient and disconnected from the mainland's power grid.

The town also invested in sustainable food production and storage. The Land Use Partnership Initiative and the popular food-to-table movement already were well established on Nantucket by 2020. There was also a successful farm-to-school program that engaged students in experiential learning opportunities while also providing fresh produce to the schools.

The islanders were cultivating new farmlands, some of them based on their ancestors' agrarian past. They made investments in livestock as well as their seafood resources. Their 50-year old recycling center continued to lead the nation in its efficiency and environmental integrity. And they maintained their natural water table beneath the island's topsoil – the ancient glacier's gift of an aquifer. Nantucket's water had a reputation for great taste and clarity.

But decades of commercial growth, mansions and estates strained the natural resources of the tiny island. Despite its well-endowed and maintained land trusts and conservation properties, as well as resurgence in the growing agricultural community, the impact of the incoming cars and trailer-trucks, construction requirements and throngs of tourists challenged the island's resources. And the island was experiencing dangerous erosion of its beaches, a result of extreme weather conditions and the rising, warming ocean.

Town leaders identified an opportunity to assess Nantucket's status in the 21st Century, as well as its increasing vulnerabilities. They assembled a team of scientists, municipal leaders and business professionals to consider ways that patterns of risks and potential benefits on the island were shifting due to population influences as well as climate change. The team proposed that the impacts and risks related to climate change could be reduced and managed through adaptation, mitigation and cost-effective solutions.

Nantucket residents embraced a newly found independence and structure for survival, based on sustainability and affordability. And the artists captured it all for posterity.

Environmentalists began working with the weight and flexibility of graphene as one of several applied applications in the Nantucket Independent Colony Model program, adding vital elements to Nantucket's energy and architectural strength. Just one-atom thin, graphene substrate enabled the integration of photovoltaic technology in conjunction with Nantucket's historic architecture, allowing solar power generation to be a transparent and invisible part of island roofs, while being aesthetically compliant with the architectural requirements of the island's Historic District Commission. This development, along with the eventual elimination of carbon-based fuels on the island, brought significant national and international attention to the Nantucket community.

Climate change took an increasing toll around the Earth as well as the island. Erosion continued to eat away at the shorelines. Predictions that Nantucket would be under water in 400 years began to take on a day-to-day reality. The historic Sankaty Lighthouse, built in 1850, finally lost ground to an ever-approaching cliff edge on the island's east coast, despite years of intensive effort and investment to save it.

The lighthouse wasn't the only loss, as the waters rose and the erratic weather brought hurricane strength winds and blizzards that threatened structures and trees and created unmanageable snow drifts in winter. Repeated flooding in the town's historic harbor challenged the viability of the wharfs and infrastructure, and increasingly extended into the town's streets, gardens and yards.

By 2050, even with the success of their technological advancements, the people of Nantucket no longer focused on development and commercialization but, rather, on survival. They were determined to maintain an independent, historically genuine and sustainable community until it was no longer possible.

The shrinking 10-mile island was attracting climatologists, scientists, agricultural productivity specialists and space explorers, rather than tourists and wealthy summer people. Electric transports powered by locally produced battery packs replaced all gas guzzling cars and trucks. Many of the mansions and estates became institutes and training centers – experiments in "living on the land," as some people referred to them. Nantucket's Independent Colony Model program served as a microcosm for communities everywhere – including Mars.

**Independence Base, 2070**

Nantucket's FPG energy technology system had transferred directly to the subterranean eddy currents on Mars, enabling operations at the first base on the planet in 2030. With maturing systems now functioning in the support infrastructure for energy, food production and closed-loop environmental systems, technology continues to evolve and advance their output as well as applications in 2070.

The stimulating problem-solving community provides a rich source of new approaches for rapidly developing prototype systems, demonstrating key capabilities and validating operational concepts. A science and technology center supports the development of new products and applications in situ, allowing for testing and production to evolve within the constraints and requirements of the Mars environment.

Engineers and architects work together using the lightweight, flexible graphene, enhanced with capabilities for protection from radiation, dust storms and meteor impacts. They have learned to combine graphene with advanced composite materials. Using their own 3D printing construction process, the teams are now able to provide most of the physical infrastructure of the growing Independence Base colony, both above and below the Mars surface.

Two thousand people are living and working on Mars. The population represents a diversity of many backgrounds in nationality, interests, experience, expertise and age, including a small young group of first generation Mars natives. The culture and social fabric of Independence Base is based on the founding principals of Nantucket Island – exhibiting the strength, leadership, tolerance, solidarity and integrity that allowed the community to live and thrive on the tiny island, independent of the American mainland.

The Nantucket House welcomes people from the island to live and work among the Mars colonists, sharing lessons learned about survivability, resourcefulness, sustainability, adaptation, vulnerability, conservation and resilience. A reciprocal center, The Mars House, is based on Nantucket, providing a continuous exchange of cultural and technical evolution, ideas and solutions for the future – on Earth and on Mars. People have learned they have a profound impact on their environment. Ultimately, the shared values of the people on both planets prove essential for survival.

## Epilogue

By the year 2400, Nantucket Island has long succumbed to Earth's rising seas, along with other islands on Earth. A billion people continue to live with unceasing climate change on what's left of the planet's continents. A million people are living on Mars, in communities of active participants, decision-makers and drivers of their destiny. Populations on Earth and Mars coexist, both striving for survival in challenging environments, taking nothing for granted. And they explore, in search of food, shelter, knowledge and a new way of life. Collaboration and innovation rule the day.

# 9. BIG GIRL

**By K. Miller**

As she wiggled her toes, the sand beneath her feet felt warm and enveloping yet the water around her was cold by contrast and made the hairs on her legs stand up. She walked farther and farther away from the shore and she could still hear the marimba's playing at the beach club behind her. As she moved along a wave began to surge in front of her suddenly carrying her to brush up against her father. He was standing his ground against the sea holding her little brother up high above the breaking waves.

He said, "Careful mind where you're goin' Sissy."

She reached up for him but he turned away saying, "You are too old". She retreated a bit and put her head back, letting her feet leave the sand and felt the water buoy her up to float along the surface of the waves. As she looked up at the bright blue sky, she felt the sea wrap its arms around her softly rocking her. With each surging wave she imagined the pounding sound of a mother's heartbeat, like an unborn child safe and warm in his mother's womb.

Just then she heard her father call, "We're leaving, hurry up and swim to shore."

She was a good swimmer after summer's on Nantucket but the waves kept crashing over her head causing her to tumble under. Each time she came up for air she could just see her father as he walked up the shore holding her little brothers hand. He stopped to glance back at her, raising his hand to signal her to hurry up. The sun was hot in the cloudless sky when she made it to the shore; she dried off quickly walking up the white sandy beach. The waves made a quiet sound as she walked away like someone calm and resting, just like breathing in and out. She looked back over her shoulder to see a family with children playing on the beach. The father looked up from the book he was reading and called out to her, "Are you ok". She smiled and nodded in response then turned back towards the hotel to go and wash up for dinner.

The bungalow her family had rented smelled of scotch and peanuts; the adults were having cocktails before dinner. Sissy could hear her little brother getting a bath and went to the room they shared to get out her clean clothes. She wasn't surprised that her clothes were all ready laid out with the shoes lined up neatly at the foot of the bed. As she stared at the clothing selection she took a deep breath and let out a long sigh, as she knew there would be no chance of wearing something else. Although she had just turned 11 years old, she was not considered old enough to pick out clothes at the store or when dressing to go out in public. This trip was the first she had been on since passing that eventful milestone where your age is written as two numbers, a preteen. This outfit was definitely one to be worn by a child. The adults were laughing in the living room of their bungalow, something about politics. Her father lit up his pipe, took a puff and then walked outside talking quietly to one of the military officers there for his meeting. Sissy peered around the doorway of her room to observe the woman laughing and drinking. Most of them had short hair and tight dresses on, fitted and low-cut on the top. They wore silk stockings and high-heeled shoes with pointy toes and a few were smoking cigarettes. They were talking about the entertainment at the dinner club and wondering if they served cocktails. There was a sitter minding the other children who saw Sissy peering around the corner and stood up to walk towards her. She said, "I heard that you will be joining them for dinner". Sissy nodded her head to say yes with a hesitation. She was too old to stay with the other children but too young to be stuck with the adults.

Sissy put on the church dress that had been laid out for her and one old petticoat to help the skirt stick out. She put on her white socks and folded them over to show the lacy edges and then buckled up her black Mary Jane shoes. Everyone was ready to walk to the dinner club. As the woman picked up their handbags and wraps and headed out the door, Sissy watched the way they walked in their high heels. They picked their legs up and put each foot down carefully flat on the floor. She looked down at her feet to the shoes with straps and no heels. She hid behind a door until they had all left and went to her parent's room. In her mother's suitcase she found a small pair of scissors, just what she needed. Sissy unbuckled each shoe and took them off. She held the scissors in one hand as she studied the first shoe. She found the spot and carefully cut the strap off of the shoe. She repeated the procedure on the second shoe. She slipped the shoes back on and she stood up to take a look in a long mirror behind the door. She smiled at the reflection of a girl that looked so much older now with grown up shoes. She dashed out the door and down the path to the dinner club where she could hear Calypso music playing on the beach.

There were many people at the outdoor dinner club, crowded around tables with white linens laughing and drinking. A group of Jamaican musicians were setting up their instruments on the beach. They were all dressed in white with a picture of palm trees embroidered on their shirts with no collars. The family Sissy saw at the beach that day was all crowed around a table eating their dinner. The father was old with grey hair and his wife looked young and pretty. Several children were out of their seats crowded around their father laughing and holding his arm. They tried several times to pull him onto the dance floor finally giving up to dance amongst themselves. Sissy recalled one time when she had danced with her father several years earlier. She saw her father wave and gesture for her to come sit down. She walked slowly towards their table hoping someone would notice how different she looked.

There was a shrimp cocktail and a Shirley Temple drink at the one empty seat at a large table. The band started playing musical games like the Limbo and several tipsy ladies got up to play. Sissy's mother noticed that she had arrived and came over to review dinner rules.

She flagged a waiter to freshen up everyone's drinks and then bent down to whisper in Sissy's ear, "Dear do you see the Grey haired man over there? He used to be a very famous actor, you know who he is don't you"?

Sissy had no idea; he just looked like a father. Her mother said well its Charlie Chaplin. The other woman at the table overheard and started new conversations about movie stars and looked around for whom else they might spot at the dinner club. Just then a photographer walked up to the table and tried to take her father's picture. Some men turned him away saying no pictures were allowed.

The band stopped playing to announce a slow dance, lady's choice. One of the tipsy lady's at her table gave Sissy a shove out of her chair and said go ask someone to dance. She stood there uncomfortably for a moment and then headed over to Mr. Chaplin's table.

She walked over to one of his son's and whispered, "Would you like to dance with me?"

The boy made a face and turned away saying, "No."

She glanced back to see her father excusing himself from the table to go speak privately with some other men.

Mr. Chaplin called to her and said, "Is that man your father"?

She nodded, and turned to walk away.

Just then Mr. Chaplin got up and said, "He must be someone very important but a lady shouldn't be left standing alone at a party."

He took her hand and walked her out on the dance floor. They danced a slow dance while cameras flashed and people pointed and stared.

Mr. Chaplin whispered, "I like your shoes" and spun her around one last time.

## A Creationist in the Dinosaur Hall

**By Amy Jenness**

Up, up to the top floor
to see the dinosaurs
The eight year old boy
will not ride an elevator
We climb
through overheated museum layers
the ocean, the land, animals, man
past family clusters
drifting on the steps
youngsters at the top
impatiently wait for the rest

And finally the raptor room
the dinosaur hall

Giddy children brush my leg
they zig zag like minnows
We wander
under hanging skeletons
past still life scenes
teeth, tusk, rib overhead
club feet down below

"I guess Creationism is dead"
Her tense angry hiss startles me
I turn
but she has left the hall
sidestepping the frothy
wash of excited children
pondering T. Rex's teeth

The eight year old boy
falls asleep in the car.
We drive
through a writhing city
of upright people in
motion on bikes, skates
running, walking

Going up the parkway
I consider the rib she said
I descend from
Sunday School
The Golden Rule

## 10. UNCHAINED

**By Charles A. Manghis**

The boy looked at the links of the chain around his wrists and the heavy lug machine bolt and nut assembly which locked it all to him. The chain ran through the old silver steam radiator and looped through the embossed cast iron. He could lean against the behemoth as it was May and had been still and silent nearly a month now.

April had been unseasonably warm and this day was splendid, the first beach day of the year for sure. They had all gone ahead to Dionis a long ride in his father's open truck. His brothers, sisters, and mother with his father driving hard bitten over the washboard roads to the Sound, but Andrew had nothing more than the chain and the radiator.

He knew the bolt kept him there. All he had done was for once not cut the grass in Mrs. Swain's field, not gathering the fresh cut hay for Bossy, his father's Jersey-Guernsey mix cow. He always collected the grass, put it in the hay wagon and brought it home...but not this one time. His father had been livid at the insubordination. Andrew had played sandlot baseball that day instead with his chums from all around the five corners.

It had felt great, early spring on Nantucket a tattered old baseball cover held on with black cloth electrical tape and his boys. Much better than the reel mower, bit dumb, heavy and slow. Andrew spent the whole afternoon imagining himself as Ty Cobb, The Babe, and a raft of his other heroes in the pantheon of his beloved American League.

For that afternoon he wasn't a poor kid in worn-out hand-me-down shoes, patched coveralls, and a too large shirt from his brother Harry. He was, well, he was chained to the steam radiator with no chance of escape.

His father had gone to the old Maxwell truck, fetched up the chain, and set him there to think about what he had done. Andrew wanted to correct him and say, "What I hadn't done," but knew better than that. His mother begged and plead with her husband not to do this, to chain their boy like a dog or a goat, wrong to tether him to a mass of cast iron, working or not.

The Old Man had done it anyway and no amount of words from Ourania could change his stubborn and set mind. Andrew was stuck and he knew it. What he didn't know was that in less than five months, the Old Man would be dead, struck down with TB and Andrew would actually wish to be chained to safety in the parlor.

One the way to Dionis Beach with all the kids in the Maxwell truck, Ourania tried every which way she could. The silent treatment, sullen and cold while her husband bade her to sing those pretty songs she trilled at the soapstone sink while washing the dinner dishes. Ourania would have no part now. When that didn't work, she tried to advocate for the boy, then reason with her husband. Finally, she grabbed the gearshift, grinding the gears and bringing the old workhorse to an abrupt halt.

"I will not go one foot further with you. If there's a fire in that house, our boy will be burnt to a cinder and it will be your fault. I've lost two children, my first Andrew and Sweet Bessie – Goddamn you, I won't lose my Andrew in chains at our home while you ask me to sing you a sweet song."

The Old Man was angry, but more shocked that his woman had been so firm and forceful. She had deigned to touch the mechanisms of this truck, and to tell him what to do. She had in fact actually issued him an ultimatum in front of their children. Almost without thinking further, the Old Man put the Maxwell in reverse backing the rear wheels into the soft shoulder sand and began slowly the humpety-bump road back to Chicken Hill.

There would be no rice pudding, potato salad or fatty bluefish grilling on the beach. The picnic had been terminated – just like that. Ourania said not a word, nor did anyone, until they reached the house. She slammed the truck door, went around back, and as she went by Bossy's pen, she stepped in a black wet cow patty and went down twisting her ankle. Ourania got up lightheaded with pain, kicked off her shoes and leapt up the steps, worried

## The Moving Pen

about Andrew and caring not for the white heat now emanating from her left foot.

She was relieved when she saw him. He had taken a broom, used it to poke and coax the newspaper off the edge of the table in the parlor. He had laid it across the floor reading the broadsheet, all elbows and knees. She saw how skinny he was, thought about how all of her children had enough to eat but barely enough. There was never money for a little more. She grew all her own vegetables, canning them in the Fall for the long winter. Ourania had her eggs too, and many fat Rhode Island Red laying hens. She mused that she had now herself become one of the hens, now actually the oldest of them all. She had no more eggs in her now. Bourne nine, lost two and here was her boy Andrew with a chain around him. Enough was enough, she would take no more of the madness. There was no way out, divorce wasn't even a word she could say out loud, fathom in its mystery or negotiate in her own way. She was chained very much like her sweet boy. The difference was that his chain would be removed by the Old Man at some point very soon. Hers were long lasting, permanent and she carried them like that character in "A Christmas Carol" by Dickens.

Andrew saw his mother, brightened and smiled, revealing his gap-toothed grin, broad and remarkable, considering his circumstances. He never complained, even when he had a toothache, stomach cramps, or growing pains. He would lay his head on his mother's ample bosom, feeling her heartbeat and she would stroke his forehead. They had an unspoken language, pure and only as a fortunate child could have with a true mother, who loved all her babies.

The Old Man came in with a pipe wrench. Ourania saw him, beat a quick exit down the hall, hobbling the best she could with the now dulling ache in her ankle. She didn't wish to have her husband further inflamed, knowing that if he had the wrench, she would prefer that he use it on the offending bond holding her son rather than on her or Andrew himself.

The Old Man said not a word as he bit into the bolt, loosening it with each turn. Neither did Andrew looking away at the cast Iron embossing "Heatilator Co Inc. Muncie Indiana USA" written along the side of the stolid silver radiator. The wrench finally loosened the shackle and the Old Man muttered, "Thank your Mother, not me. I'd a kept you in this a good goddamn long time till you do what I tell you to do."

Andrew nodded assent and quickly got out of the way of the huge wrench. He was free. There were marks on his skinny forearm from the links, but they would soon fade away. He realized how hungry he was and thought of his mother's picnic basket, meant earlier for Dionis beach and his family. He went past the battered the Maxwell and saw the basket in the open bed of the truck. Andrew opened the crockery and Anchor hocking glassware his mother got as promotions during her one extravagance, a weekly trim to the Dreamland Theatre to watch the talkies for a nickel. There were buttermilk biscuits and a pile of fried chicken in a crock. Andrew took with both hands, then put most back, realizing his siblings share was in his hands too. He was a fair boy, never cunning or mean like many of his classmates in his fourth grade class. He would have been described as guileless by his favorite teacher, Miss Folger.

After his mother, Andrew thought Miss Folger was the nicest woman in the whole wide world. Her hair was perfectly bobbed and pinned up, and she faintly smelled of lilac and rosewater. When Andrew went to her desk to turn in his work papers or penmanship, he would secretly inhale deeply to take in that pleasant aroma at her desk. He would recall her scent many times during the day, most especially after a confrontation or any danger of any matter. It would help to recenter and relax him from any tumult or fear.

He walked down Chicken Hill and passed the Old Mill. Old Man Rebimbas waved to him, his cows grazing lazily around the structure and millstone. Andrew waved back then threw the chicken leg bone into the ditch alongside the back of the Old Mill. A shiny black crow flapped, cackled, and picked it up a mere second after it had hit the clover. Seemed nothing was wasted these days. Even the crows knew that.

There was still a hefty chunk of ice in Ourania's icebox. She took a claw hammer from the oak Hoosier cabinet and cracked off a good chunk from the block. Wrapped in a dishtowel, she tied it to her ankle so that she could continue her never-ending series of chores.

The Summer people she would be cleaning for next month would have described her work as drudgery. She prided herself on keeping her home clean and tidy with a brood and passel of children seemingly hell bent to undo every one of her good works. Her daughter Helen and little Mary would soon enough begin to help her, and learn all the practical and necessary things to do.

She would send all her children out with Eight O'clock Coffee cans from the A&P. She would punch holes at 12 and 6 o'clock with a long string tied through to go over each child's neck. That would free up both of their hands to pick fat blackberries drooping down from their canes, laden with sweet purple fruit. He children's fingers and mouths would be stained deep purple, as they ate as much as they desired, later pooping purple, seedy stools early and often. Ourania would save her egg money and Mrs. Ramos and Ourania would buy and split a two-hundred pound bag of sugar from the baker, in order to put up much blackberry jam.

Ourania made the best preserves on the Island, bar none. Her hidden ingredient was crushed spearmint leaves boiled into the mass of purple fruit. One couldn't put their finger or tongue on it, but it made her blackberry preserves absolutely marvelous. She would cut the mint from her herb garden, far from Bossy's pen and slyly add it. She did something similar with her pear jam too. They didn't own a pear tree, but there was an ancient and hoary old tree at the edge of the Quaker Cemetery. Ourania would send the boys with a wagon to pick several hundred pounds of ripe pears, and seed and core for days. Her pear jam secret was ground crushed clove...an expensive but effective choice to make all tongues that tasted it wag with delight.

Nantucket's tongues wagged incessantly at the slightest sidestep or misdemeanor, real or imagined. Lord knows there were plenty of both. Ourania felt empowered over all the tongues, as if her kitchen concoctions held them all at bay controlling them and keeping them from flapping at will. She had tamed them, owned them, her name was on their palate, and there was nothing but sweetness and a certain tang.

Ourania sold a fair share of her jams and was careful to secret the money, along with her egg money from her husband. She would dip into it from time to time in order to buy extras for her children at Ashley's Market or the A&P. She was tempted on occasion with a pretty hat or a smart pair of kit gloves from the Jenny Lind Shop on Petticoat Row. But she never gave into the temporary lust for style and beauty.

Once she tried on a coat, making a show of having her money showing so the German lady owner would have to take it out of the window, sensing a pending sale in the works. Ourania tried it on, looked approvingly at herself in the three-sided mirror, then quickly made the sour-puss pucker she had practiced stating, "The cut wasn't quite right on her." Ourania then ceremoniously placed the beautifully tailored wool coat over her right arm and carefully handed it back to Frau Remsler. "I'll come back when you have something more suited to my taste...Good day, Mrs. Remsler and thank you."

Ourania again felt empowered. Her money hadn't been spent on such a beautiful coat and would never be. But indeed for that moment, it could have been at fat Frau Remsler nearly treated Ourania with the respect she craved. Ourania realized the merchant did not care or have any sense of fealty for her, only for the healthy respect of her purse. Ourania kept that respect for herself, holding it close, knowing she'd need it, but not knowing when.

Andrew knew not to make the grass-cutting mistake again. His father was right – the chain had taught Andrew a lesson. He rolled the reel mower down the hill, cut and raked the field in record time. The hay wagon would be rolled down, filled, and set for Bossy to eat great amounts from. Bossy in turn did her part by producing warm rich milk laden with heavy cream. Andrew milked then filled two clean milk bottles and walked to Mrs. Swain's.

He left the two quart bottles on a shady stoop high enough and hidden to keep away cats and any incidental sneak thief. Mrs. Swain oft times gave him a homemade ginger cookie or lemon square, but today she was nowhere to be seen. He might have left the bottles in her icebox, but she had King, a mean old hunting dog with one eye totally white and blasted. King sensed Andrew's fear each time and would get up and bay blazes at him. Scared him some good. It was during times like that, that Andrew would hearken back and recall Miss Folger's sweet scents. He would be calm and fine by the next block of houses. Worked every time.

The Old Man drove his truck onto the steamer *Gay Head* bound for New Bedford. Three times a month, weather permitting, he drove the truck always full of what needed to be hauled off the Island, for whomever needed a carter to do so.

The Old Man always came back with the same load, without fail. He brought huge loads of very hard, very green bananas still on their stalk. Some of them were taller than him at 6'2", often outweighing his 175 pounds by nearly half again. He carefully loaded them tossed to him by the stevedores in New Beige, as the Portagees called New Bedford. The stevedores were all Irish and Cabo Verde – Cape Verdeans from Brava or the other dusty islands off the West African Coast. The Old Man called out in Creolu to Reynaldo, the boss, "Get your boys and you Micks over to the Maxwell, I need to be on the late boat, need to get outta New Beige and get home to Nantucket."

Reynaldo was missing his four front teeth, two top, two bottom, and stuck out an enormously long tongue through the opening thereby making the best obscene gesture the Old Man had ever seen. It looked exactly like a big fat beet red cock erect and ready for a hard plowing. Reynaldo did it each time he saw the Nantucketer and it made the Old Man snort and chortle without fail.

"Ok, old man, grab onto this, an I will bring 'dem over there. Bring me one of 'dem Nantook Sallys and she not go back to that Island home again. Once she rides with Reynaldo, she stay in Ne Beige fo'ever."

"Now that's enough, you black bastard," the Old Man chimed back. "You got that tongue, but that's all you got, the waterfront girls have all told me that. Now get your Micks and boys and get me my turbanas...Enough of your bullshit, Reynaldo."

"Ok, Ok, Old Man. Pay up Manny in the United Fruit warehouse. Give Reynaldo your paper and we bang out your work."

As the bananas were loaded, a couple of giant cockroaches scurried into the Maxwell before the Old Man could get them with his boot heel. Once, on Island, he found one torpid with cold in October. They were the size of sparrows and crunched loudly underfoot. He had disturbing visions of them making a new home on Chicken Hill, but realized the rainforests outside Managua were their true home and Nantucket would never be.

When he got the bananas across the Sound and back on island, he went to work getting them into the cobwebbed basement of the A&P. He figured he might get 3½ cents per pound for this lot before his expenses. He still had to buy the ethylene gas to turn the dark green fruit lighter green, from which they would soon quickly ripen to sweet yellow sugar tubes. Nantucketers had taken quickly to the Old Man's new produce, it had been a sensation to them, and Mr. Sylvia at the A&P promised to sell every last one of the turbanas. "We will take all you will bring us, Harry," he repeated over and over when he first tasted the finished product, over three years ago.

Nantucketers were a queer mixture of the cosmopolitan and the xenophobe. They had first gotten a taste of the exotic during the first whaling voyages. Sugar cane, silk, coconuts, tapioca, ginger, all strange commodities, and they had found an enthusiastic home in the Islanders larder. Later the Portagees brought linguica, kale, wines, chourizo, and all their 'Gee food from Fayal and Madeira. But old habits died hard. Cornmeal, molasses, smoked fish, hardtack, potato and white onion, the bland staples of the Yankee diet often made the unexciting and uninspired dishes of their forbearers.

These bananas had taken off in a big way on the Island. Some of the country bumpkins thought the bitter skin was to be eaten, like an apple. They sliced the bananas in a log-like manner and proceeded to attempt to eat it whole. But that was early on and now even a Polpis schoolboy bit off the stem and quickly unzipped the unexpected sweetness inside the bitter yellow skin. The Old Man had finally turned a corner. He didn't own pasture, a dairy farm like the Jaeckle sisters in Somerset or the Bartlett spread close by them, growing vegetables and flowers for the summer visitors. The Old Man had a banana farm, growing out of the rusty freighter from Managua or Guatemala land. He was on his way – he would give the coofs from away a run for their New York and Philadelphia money. Harry – The Old Man – Turbana King of Nantucket Island.

He noticed the raspy morning cough that wouldn't end soon after his five a.m. rising time. He would cough into his handkerchief first pink rose, then bright red. The Old Man would sputter, cough, see trails and steady himself. He wasn't yet 35, not yet grey, stooped or bent. He wasn't in his prime, having worked hard, drank hard, and lived hard, especially before Ourania. He was prone to fits of rage and sometimes extreme cruelty. His friends had taunted him as a boy, one stating that he was "raised by wolves." He had blackened Eben Gardner's eyes, both of them, and cracked his ribs too, for good measure.

Eben hadn't been much off track. The Old Man had been raised by wolves and he was no Romulus or Remus either. He had done his best to try to forget, did it with a taste of the creature, mostly Rum, but had even used and taken Laudanum when he could get his hands on some. He had cleaned up mostly after little Bessie had died, and the first Andrew soon after had made him not so much a changed man as an altered one. He slowly began to focus on his family's future and not the tortured crawl of his childhood, and not into the even more descending despair of those teenage years. He had escaped the chains by signing up for Woodrow Wilson's great adventure in Europe in 1917. He was gassed horribly for the favor at the battle of the Meuse-Argonne Forest and even worse at Verdun. The Huns had nearly killed him, but he slowly and painfully recovered, half blinded and lungs almost turned inside out.

He got back to Boston in 1918, and then almost died again of the Spanish Flu during the pandemic. He pulled a second u-turn in front of the grim Reaper, who had wanted his boy, sorry ass, but the Old Man had run hard and wasn't ready to give it up to him just yet. It was then that he went from being strong strapping in his prime, to being the Old Man then not even thirty years old. He had fought, clambered, and crawled back to Nantucket, but after watching the millworkers in Lawrence and Lowell eating bananas daily in their lunch bucket, he learned how the importers and shippers worked the Boston, Lowell, Lawrence run and was determined to do the same from new Beige over to Nantucket.

Once he figured it out and done his homework up north, he set back to New Bedford and much to his chagrin found a Frenchman named Jules LaRocque who had a strong-arm tether on the trade there. The Old Man hung out, studied the wharves, terrain, players, and waited. He first tried to ease his way into LaRocque's fiefdom, but had no success. The Old Man was not a man used or prone to diplomacy or kind words and hadn't had the skills to come up with a business partnership even if LaRocque had wished for a new partner in his enterprise.

What the Old Man still possessed was lightning fast reflexes and a rapier uppercut and a pair of fists that demolished anything that got in his way. Once Jules LaRocque was knocked down, he was quickly disabled with sharp swift kicks to his side. This was done with dispatch, the whole business taking no more than thirty seconds. The Frenchman was two inches taller and fifty pounds heavier but had never stood a chance. The Old Man had worked him like a snowy owl on a Coatue rabbit. LaRocque went back to Quebec by train, hiring two bodyguards to help him board and ward off any further violence from his unseen assailant. The Old Man had his pass, his token of the pass, and would now fiercely guard and hold onto it. He quickly hired several of LaRocque's men, with promises of a better cut of the turbana trade. They knew what had become of their former employer and hadn't realized that the Old Man was indeed his own muscle. They all thought he had an empire and they didn't realize that indeed they were right. They were his empire, his unknowing minions. It was built upon the foundation of fear, ignorance, and the desire for more and better. It was actually working for all of them in different ways, different reasons, different seasons.

His blood was now deep royal crimson and the entire family was fearful. Ourania boiled everything to kill the germs, towels, handkerchiefs, even the sheets that the Old Man slept in. Andrew stayed farther away, guilty of thoughts that he now didn't ever have to fear the chain and lug bolt. He still dutifully mowed Mrs. Swain's field for the grass, but now because his family deprived of his father's cartage and turbana income seemed further and further behind. Every movement the Old Man made reminded Andrew of a death rattle. His father swayed unsteadily when he made any effort to walk, now like a scarecrow blowing in a stiff northeast wind. Andrew and his older brother, Harry, began picking up other odd jobs when they could, now bringing the stray dimes and quarters to Ourania. Her trips to Petticoat Row had stopped months earlier. The Old Man needed help for nearly everything now – even trips to the bathroom. He had stopped conversing now just barely uttering a grunt or uhhhhnnn, in order to affirm yes that he did need water, food, or to take a piss. Unlike most TB patients, the Old Man passed quickly. Perhaps because of the poisons in Europe, the hard-lived years before and after, or a combination of all the cumulative assaults on himself. The Old Man shed his mortal coil on New Year's Day 1930.

The economic panic which had shaken New York, Boston, Philadelphia, and now the entire world now finally settled in on the small island. When it had begun in late September 1929, most of the Summer people had already left, taking with them most of the money and real jobs until the following June when the cycle would reestablish itself. 1929 was an unusually snowy and cold winter. The coal stove in the parlor glowed and the children piled under wool blankets and ancient comforters after dinner as the house was very chilly and draft prone. Harry had begun shoveling coal from the barges that tied up alongside Commercial Wharf under the watchful eye of Old Man Killen and was allowed to take home whatever was strewn around the wharf at the end. It was back-breaking, dirty, hard work and Harry worked alongside husky and bearded Charlie Sayle. He had taken Harry on when he learned of the Old Man's passing due to the TB. Andrew also asked Charlie for work but there were grown men with families to feed in need of wages. Harry would have to do for now.

His sister Helen had gotten a commitment for a cleaning-boarding-companion position in 'Sconset. There was an invalid widow in one of Mr. Underwood's cottages on McKinley Street. Miss Ida Roberts was one of the heirs to a vast timber fortune wrested from west of the Rockies fifty years ago. She was now too sick to return to Villanova, Pennsylvania and took Helen on for a small salary. Helen promptly left school, set out for 'Sconset, and moved into a small room in the cottage. 'Sconset was a world away from her family and her home on Chicken Hill and she cried nightly wishing for her mother and siblings. To make matters worse, Miss Ida had hardening of the arteries, or dementia as they said, and she bade Helen a different name each time she saw her. Miss Ida was sweet until the sun went down, but in the evenings turned angry and feral. She would get combative and agitated and Helen worried that the old bird would lash out and strike her, but she never did.

Helen had figured out how best to mollify the old girl sometimes with a nice pan of baked codfish or a hearty chowder made with the sea clams washed up at 'Sconset beach after a nor'east blow. Helen had learned to cook at the right hand of Ourania and made her dishes just as her mother had taught her. There were no real stores out there; and once a week, Helen would ride into town with the Postmaster and go to Ashley's or the A&P for foods she couldn't get from neighbors further up in 'Sconset. She even got the dairy from the old farmer in Quidnet along the milk run. Fresh butter, cream, milk, and rich farmer cheese was a welcome treat. Helen put a few pounds on her rail-thin frame. She felt healthy and strong if exiled out on her east-end perch.

Her family held together, cobbling together work, food opportunity, and luck as they found them. Ourania had made a plan to rent out the Old Man's former sick room. She had aired, boiled, and disinfected with bottles of Lysol. She took in a big, lumpy, Irish laborer named McNally Dowling. She had checked him out thoroughly and while not as sober as a judge, he was a man with scruples, a kind heart and a wild sense of humor, one like she had not ever seen before.

He was employed cutting in mosquito ditches through a Federal WPA project in Madaket. McNally would regale her little ones with slapping bugs the size of ravens in Galway. He made Ourania's children sing with delight as they followed him up Chicken Hill on his way home from work with a Mary Jane or Tootsie Roll for each and every one of them on his payday, Thursdays.

The Old Man had never endeared himself nor engendered any goodwill to his children the way this big Irishman had. They had feared and respected the Old Man but had never truly loved him. Ourania had wished on occasion to inquire whether McNally Dowling had left a stout wife and children of his own back on Galway's rocky coast. She thought the better of it, but always wondered why this man had landed here on Nantucket of all places in the Spring of 1930? How had he landed a job on the WPA when the agent saw to it that names like Coffin, Folger, Swain, Worth, and Gardner were chosen? Nantucketers called his kind "bog walkers," even and while there were no external signs of intolerance here, no NINA (or No Irish Need Apply) signs like in the store windows of New Beige. Nonetheless McNally Dowling had a dollar a week for his room and every dollar helped feed, clothe, warm, and otherwise care for her brood during that hungry and harsh year of 1930.

With the coming of spring, Andrew hunted wild asparagus knowing each and every choice patch that grew year to year. He and his brother

Teddie found tender fiddleheads, watercress and snatched fat bullfrogs for their meaty hind legs. Pickerel and white perch came from Miacomet and Hummock Pond, and Ourania fried them up pin leaf lard and the crackling brown fillets were gobbled up as fast as they were fried in Ourania's cast iron skillet on the range oil stove.

The Old Man was never spoke of – although little Mary often asked why there were no more sweet yellow bananas to eat. No one around the old oak table said a word and Mary ate another fish filet washed down with chocolate milk.

McNally had presented Ourania with a little, round, brown can labelled Hershey's Chocolate Syrup. No one saved it for the chocolate sheet cake Ourania had baked for Mary – today was her fifth birthday. Her mother had done up Mary's hair like Shirley Temple in the movies and she was indeed a princess that evening. There were five little pink twisted wax candles dribbling onto the frosting and Mary blew and spit at the same time. Everyone tried their best not to notice and looked away before the big applause and foot stomping after Happy Birthday was sung again with much bravado and zeal. Ourania cut the cake into generous slabs and there was not a sound other than forks clinking alongside the dessert plates. Harry pronounced this the best meal his mother had ever made – though he said that just about every evening whether the meal was a feast or more humble fare.

He, like Andrew, kept a fairly sunny disposition, never complaining about the hard work, long hours, or short wages they earned. Her boys hadn't been saints by any means, but they hadn't been RBW or raised by wolves...Ourania had seen to that no matter what and the end result were her sons. She had managed through incredible odds against her to break the chain. She had done it several times when her overall presence and voice were not up to the powers against her. Through her perseverance, wit, and faith in herself, and her children, she managed to make it out - sometimes bent, but never broken.

The Old Man was lying in repose in the Old North Burying ground. Ourania thought she was in some sense better off and in others worse off without him. She knew not what lay ahead, and her life had been a constant river of toil, heartache and trouble, but with each and every baby she had borne came a bright burning ember to lighten the darkness and gloom around her. Each new life brought her the tiny pink fingers, beautiful repose of the sleeping face, and the latching and gentle suckling to her breast. She guided each one of them from needful and helpless infants, to tentative, inquisitive toddlers, then to school age and beyond. Every one of her children who had survived had turned into tough and determined but sweet little weeds, always managing to poke through the cracked cement sidewalks and well-trod cobblestones. They all showed off their flower topped caps, which blew back and forth in the breezes which were the travails of their Island lives. As with those weeds springing from between the cobblestones, the winds of tumult somehow stiffened their stalk spines and in spite of those winds, they sprouted new smiles each day like the new flower petals on their weedy heads.

Ourania thought all about this as she picked those tender dandelion greens which had not yet sprouted flowers. They were soft and tender much like her first Andrew and baby Bessie. God had taken them to his heavenly throne, perhaps because of their baby-soft tenderness which would support the heavenly Father in His infinite and eternal dotage. She had wailed for weeks after little Bessie's passing, only six weeks old cold and lifeless, in the wooden cradle Ourania's father had crafted for her and her eleven siblings. Each and every one of them had been rocked in that cradle, as had Ourania's own babies afterwards.

It had been a gift from her mother when Ourania announced her engagement to her husband to be. Her mother climbed up high in her barn, dusted and cleaned it for it had not been used for many years. The cradle had intricate inlays of golden whale tooth ivory, mother of pearl, tortoise shell, and the date 1864 inlaid in black baleen. The whaling voyage had kept him from the roiling bloodbath cauldron known as the War Between the States.

Ourania's father was a skilled craftsman, the ship's carpenter aboard the "Awashonks." He cruised the South Pacific in search of sperm whales during the majority of the worst of the savagery between Union and Confederate. It was in Mowee in the Sandwich Islands or Owhyhee that he cut the dense brown wood called Koa by the natives. He had crafted that beautiful cradle which would calm his unborn children and grandchildren.

# The Moving Pen

When Bessie's still body had lain in it, Ourania packed it high up in the eaves of her barn, way out of sight and when little Mary, the last of her babies came, she had lain in an open set of drawers in a heavy bureau. The Old Man asked where the 1864 was and Ourania feigned not hearing his query skimming her feather duster over mantel and Hoosier cabinet humming a little song to herself as she dusted, not hearing him. The Old Man had muttered that keeping an infant in an open set of chest drawers was crazy when the 1864 was serviceable and sturdy, but not getting an answer promptly moved on and forgot about the whole thing.

Now the Old Man was in the Old North Burying ground colder than a witch's tit, as he would have said. Ourania didn't have to listen, to obey, to kowtow to his unreasonable or brutish ways. She was free. She was frightened.

McNally Dowling had stayed with her family for nearly two years before the accident took him from them abruptly and without warning. The Madaket ditch mosquito control project was primarily done by hand cutting wide swaths of marsh in order to bring salt water to infiltrate the pools of fresh rain water kettle holes left by the receding glaciers thousands of years earlier. They were perfect breeding grounds for giant swarms of thirsty pests. Madaket in fact was a native Wampanoag word which literally meant "bad lands" and it had been so since time immemorial. Roosevelt's boys in Washington had seen fit to distribute $6000 a year throughout the 1930s in order to put Nantucket men to work cutting ditches to remediate the incessant pestilence.

McNally Dowling ran a small steam boiler stoking it with coal and constantly replenishing it with fresh water. The boiler in turn propelled a steam shovel which could do the work of a dozen laborers in one fell swoop. He kept the coal loaded, and the steam regulated, a tricky task, but one much preferred by Mr. Dowling to the muscle pulling, backbreaking cutting of the marsh. He even kept a citronella bucket candle by the machine to keep the flying eight-legged vampire bugs somewhat at bay. The same candle had somehow managed to vibrate off and land upon the open gas can used to fill the truck that took them to town. McNally never saw anything but the white flash, and the men cutting marsh saw the black cloud of thick smoke knowing there was dead trouble for the big Irishman.

Mercifully he was asphyxiated before his burning body hit the soft saltmarsh hay around him.

He had told Ourania that if anything ever happened to him the he was to be buried back in the Old Sod of Galway town. He had been emphatic, usually after a drink or two saying it over and over. "My Old Sod Galway." Ourania had bade him hush, that no good would come of talk of that kind. "Only bad luck would be assigned to talk of that order Mr. Dowling. It is not to be spoken again in my parlor or my presence."

Now Ourania was faced with another death task, her second in two years. She spoke with Lemuel Chase, who still had the old whale oil casks in his cooperage and stable, and one was delivered to the Lewis Funeral Parlor where Mr. Lewis filled it a third of the way with kosher pickling salt and then water from the harbor on Washington Street extension, round the back of the funeral parlor on Union Street. McNally Dowling was safely and securely ensconced in his briny home, bobbing in death as he had in life and even before in his mother's salty belly in Galway Town. The barrel was borne aboard a packet ship bound for New Beige and then to a steam freighter on its way to Ireland.

She had found his burlap sack with his personal effects and his money hidden in his mattress as she knew it would be there. His gold hunter's case pocket watch was faithfully wound every day and hung on a nail beside his bed. He always said the pocket watch had to remain upright and never lain down in order to keep time honest and true. There was a note in the burlap along with $153.00 in cash. Ourania unfolded the note and read his awkward scrawl, reading past the cross-outs and misspellings.

"I suppose if you are areadin' this then I am either dead or you are a sneak thief. This money and these goods belong to Mr. McNally Dowling and indeed if I am dead and gone it is to go to Mr.s Ourania Chase, for the benefit of her and her young'uns. My watch for Master Andrew, my ring for Master Harry. Be sure to buy some fine and fancy food and drink at Ashley's market and have a time for me. Pray for my eternal soul and spirit. God bless you all and God commend my body to his hevenly bower to repose in his sunshine and everlasting love.

"Your faithful servant
"McNally Dowling"

Ourania wept as she folded his papers and placed them back in the burlap. She had grown to love Mr. McNally Dowling and could not believe that he too was dead and gone. She hadn't even cried when the Old Man had finally passed. He had been dying for months and his passing came as a surprise to no one, much less Ourania as his constant caregiver and comfort at the end of his long and difficult journey.

She had grown fond of McNally, his twinkling eyes, his jolly way, the way he took such delight in bouncing little Mary on his knee or going down on all fours to give her his horsey rides, bucking gently and whinnying to make Mary chortle with delight.

The family lit candles in St. Mary's Parish Catholic Church on Federal Street. They had never set foot there before. The Old Man had called St. Mary's people "Mackerel Snappers" as they listened to his nonsensical diatribes, screeds, and polemics against all things Pope-ish. It was rumored that the Old Man's great-grandfather was a 'Gee from Pico Island in the Azores and that he had come to Nantucket aboard a whale ship in the 1820s. Why that would have made the Old Man part Mackerel Snapper himself Ourania thought. The Old Man categorically denied those claims, disputing and stating that Great-grandpa Chase was borne out on Abrams Point in the harbor near where the last Injun Abram Quary fished and hunted, last of the Mohicans he was Old Abram.

Great-grandpa was pure Nantucket native not Portagee. That was just a slur that the Coffins and Bunkers had perpetrated against the Old Man's kin. It was nothing more than bad blood he said.

So McNally Dowling was set across the Atlantic and Ourania set out to once again rearrange the tenuous unfathomable mystery that had become her existence and that of her family. . .(to be continued)

# Lyric

## by Ursula Austin

(carpenter)
wood
bending itself
By his hand
lifting  each grain
as planed pine boards
become a sepia desert
swallowed
into the clouds
of a flowering golden tree

# Lenny's Garage

## By Amy Jenness

awkward poses
wine glass chit chat
cocktail party
dancers search out
their 10 minute partners

The gala speech waltz,
welcome, intro,
thank yous
welcome, intro
thank yous

party girl selfie
livin' the life
flapper pearls and
a curved spit-curl
a harbor view

dance hall hoofer
collecting blue-blazered
men, ranking them
based on the
size of their wallets

Speeches done
I circled the room
footwork precise
head up, stomach in
I saw and was seen
now it's after
on to Lenny's garage
there's poems
bourbon and barbeque
relaxed laughter

# 11. SUNDAY

**By K. Miller**

Miss Beulah Mae had worked in our house for five years by the time I started third grade that year. She and Nana loved me so much that they never scolded me or reminded me of the rules in our house. Miss Beulah Mae was with us six days each week and I missed her terribly on Sundays. She lived out in the country in a town with no roads, just well worn paths. I had learned how to get there through the swamp and piney woods from all of her stories. I knew how to stay away from the sinkholes and gator tracks, avoid low hanging Spanish moss full of chiggers and knew the poisonous plants and snakes to avoid.

I woke up early that morning and grabbed some tangerines and put them in my red plaid lunch box. I slipped through the screen door and made my way out to the swamp. I could hear the frogs constant high-pitched croaking and a couple of coon dogs barking. I walked out to the edge of our property just in view of the swamp where I found a footpath that looked like people had walked there many times before. The underbrush was dead and flattened forming a narrow path with a carpet of pine needles stretching out into the woods. As I walked along, the path seemed to never end and I heard the sounds of bigger animals. I picked up my pace and ran until I saw a clearing through the trees. A large farm spread out at the edge of the woods with more houses in the distance. I could smell fresh cut sugar cane in the fields to my left and saw corn and melons in the fields to my right. Up ahead was a lovely old house raised up off the ground with a porch running all the way round. The tin roof was so bright in the morning sun; I had to shade my eyes to look at it.

I saw a man out on his front porch sitting on an over turned washtub cleaning his boots. I walked up and said, "Mornin Sir, do you know Miss Beulah Mae?" He said that he did and called out to someone inside the house, "Dr. Weems child is loose out here". Before I said another word, Miss Beulah Mae came running out the door and down the steps to sweep me up saying, "You like to scare me to death Missy what are you doin out here?" I told her I missed her and she said that I would have to wait till later to go home. She took a step back and then took my hand to turn me around and said, "Well I see you already dressed for church". I smiled and said, "Yes, Mame". Her family all came out to take a look at me and then we walked to church. At my church the priest only spoke in Latin and the songs were all from the hymnal behind each pew. Everyone spoke English at this church and we did more singing than listening. I got to sit on Miss Beulah Mae's lap during the talking and then each time another song started she would jump up and throw me off so that we could all clap and dance. After church there was a big supper where everyone had brought a dish. No one told me what to eat or how to eat it so I ate corn on the cob, pickles and pie until I felt sick.

When folks started walking home Miss Beulah Mae told me it was naptime and I'd best be getting home for it. She and her husband loaded me into their hay wagon and hitched up an old horse to pull us. We took a different way back to my house with a path wide enough for the wagon. As we approached the house, I could see father standing there in his scrubs and white lab coat, with that look of inconvenience due to my mother's tears and he not having all the answers. I hopped down off the wagon and Miss Beulah Mae sent me in the house while she talked with father. I was tired and took a long nap that day. When my mother woke me up she simply asked if I had had a nice visit to the farm. That was the day our black and white TV was given to the neighbors.

# 12. ALL THE WAY OUT IN 'SCONSET

**By Daryl Westbrook**

It is 2014 and one can still here the retort, "All the way out to 'Sconset."

In the late 1700's islanders built fish shacks along the eastern most shore of the island as codfish were abundant and an easy catch. The fish were filleted and preserved for the winter. When the fishing season was over, the men would leave the shacks and go back to Nantucket town.

In the mid 1800's Siasconset had enough permanent residents to have a one-room school house and a church was built, but it was still far removed from the news of the day. It was one man and his daughter who sought to remedy the distance from 'Sconset and the world. Captain Baxter and his daughter, Love, set up a mail delivery service from their cottage, Shanunga, for the village.

Captain Baxter would meet the boat coming from the mainland in his horse and carriage and return. Upon reaching the village he would start blowing his horn so that all would hear that the mail was in. One can imagine that most work was suspended and a general melee faced Captain Baxter as he came into 'Sconset. The mail brought news from loved ones whether off at Sea or on the mainland. The highlight that day was hearing the news of the town that the captain delivered along with the mail. The gathering at his house was one of great exchanges among the residents as they related the news that the mail had brought them.

Love Baxter was in charge of the mail that was being sent from the village. The cost was one cent for each piece. In 1872 Love was officially appointed by the United States government as, the first postmistress of 'Sconset. The post office location remained at the Baxter home until she retired and then moved to the bridge in 'Sconset for the next postmistress to take over. The post office was served by only women until 1949. Women were left to take care of business and home very much like when the men went off whaling. In 1949 with the war over, Philip Morris, a resident of 'Sconset, applied to be the postmaster. He owned a building in the square and it became the post office for the village. The government agreed to pay rent for the building and Philip Morris was officially appointed the postmaster. The building is the building we enjoy today as the post office.

The post office in 1949 was very much the hub of activity and news, not unlike when the Baxters distributed the mail, as there was still very little communication with the mainland. Telephone service was marginal, some radio, no television, there were newspapers brought to the island, but the congenial atmosphere of exchanging news of town and off island still occurred at the post office. Cocktails parties were the social events of the summer and getting the invitations into the hands of friends on island was a paramount responsibility of the postmaster. The task has not changed much in importance, but today, it is not as easy as in 1949. Mail service has not improved with the times. Believe it or not the mail goes off island before it goes in the box at the 'Sconset post office and then it is sorted and distributed.

The late 1800's had brought summer people with money who enjoyed the fresh ocean breeze and long sandy beach and have built wonderful summer cottages with ocean views along the bluff. It was not long before hotels were built and more people came to enjoy this setting by the sea. The visitors arrived by horse and carriage from the pier or by train. The train connected the boat with Surfside and 'Sconset. The trains offered an amazing ride along the ocean cliffs past miles of pines and grazing sheep into the remote village of 'Sconset. The fanfare of the train's arrival was always a crowd pleaser and many came to see summer visitors arrive but the anchor for the news was always the post office. The excitement and news that the train carried with it did not survive. The train tracks were taken up for the metal needed in the first world war.

With the arrival of the summer resident and visitors, the post office became even more of a bastion with the world, because residents and guests alike wanted to communicate with the mainland and others.

In 1949, the post office was opened 7 days a week for people to get mail. The number of residents owning post office boxes originally was 200, and within 5 years it was 350 families. 'Sconset was growing. The post office was an information center, employment agency, bank, lost and found department, a waiting room for the bus, a kids play area as mothers greeted each other, and incidentally, a place to buy stamps and get your mail.

In the beginning of summer it is one of the first stops to say, "Hold the mail now for P.O. box ----, we are here." Philip Morris's tenure as postmaster allowed him to know all his box holders. The tales of family and adventures over the winter had to be told by each returnee. Phil recounted when he retired that he had known some of the patrons from the time before they could reach the window at the post office until they had families of their own.

The predecessors to the job of postmaster have been equally as welcoming, but with the post office having shorter hours and many more box holders; the opportunity to have a relationship with the customer is not possible. The convenience of cell phones, internet and cable TV has taken its toll on the post office importance in the village . It is not the source of news it once was, but it is still the social gathering spot for seeing friends who just returned to the island, showing off the new grandchild or baby.

The lobby is still used as a playground as families chat, still the information center on beaches, buses and directions, lost and found postings, ticket sales for non-profit events and still stamps, albeit much fewer hours.

My personal memories of Philip Morris was his love the of Red Sox baseball team and when you went to the post office you would often hear the game playing on the radio in the back office. He was also an avid fisherman. He would brag about his catch of a bass or a bushel of quahogs, mussels or scallops but his spot was always a secret. I know more than one person who tried to find the spots but was frustrated to the end.

Jim Ozias was the next post master that I remember fondly. He had a knack of remembering everything about your family and their names and would genuinely ask about them when you returned to the island. His aptitude for remembering astonished many, I am sure.

## The Moving Pen

Karen Coffin followed in Jim's shoes and she took on the task of dealing with the public. The tourists now came in droves asking her to be the information center for Sconset and possibly the whole island. There were days when I don't think she had time to sell a stamp. Her credit was she answered every question with a smile.

The best part of talking to the post office manager was that they could always tell you immediately by looking at the back of boxes whether your friends had arrived on island. You knew that if they were on island; their post office box would be open.

How lucky we are to have 02564 - so far away from the hustle and bustle of town - "All the way out in 'Sconset."

# My Mother Didn't Tell Me

**By Kristine Glazer**

My mother didn't tell me that when I was a little girl
Dreams I dreamed then would fade from my view.

My mother didn't tell me that I would find a place, for me, far out to sea.
My mother didn't tell me that trees sometimes lift the Earth up high,
And when you walk on bricks and cobblestones you can hear the ferry's cry.

My mother didn't tell me that like the waiting in springtime
For the flowers to bloom and the birds to sing,
My expectations would always run high.

My mother didn't tell me that sometimes the wind sings and talks, all day and night.
My mother didn't tell me that when you watch the setting sun, shadows of purple and pink paint your skin.

My mother didn't tell me that cranberries can make you squeal with delight, as you watch the pale gray sky meet the golden brown earth, and the golden brown earth meet the cold blue water, and the RED cranberries rise to the top through green blades of grass, in crisp autumn air.

My mother didn't tell me that winter skies are at their finest when trees with their empty branches must stand in the wind.

My mother didn't tell me that birds have patterns
In their wakeful days and sleep-filled nights, and as fog fills the air, and sand shifts beneath the sea, my dreams are renewed.

My mother didn't tell me why she loved the birds so, but I know that she did.

## 13. RUN

**By K. Miller**

It was raining and bitter cold at night in Rungsted Kyst, a train ride away from Kobenhavn. I had chosen to move to Denmark to get away from Bruce, a pro football player/drug dealer who was very attached to me. He was my first boyfriend and I was unprepared for dealing with him. Instead of breaking up with him I decided to move. I had gotten permission to transfer to a school abroad and off I went.

I tended to protect my heart well back then. Decisions were often made quickly with little planning at the hint of danger. I wasn't prepared for the cold weather and the close-knit family I came to live with. They sat together in the evenings, in the same room to drink tea, read books and chat quietly together. When I walked to the local sweet shop and came back with a candy bar they expected that I would cut it into small pieces and share it with everyone. I was thinking to eat the whole thing on my way back home or save it in my room for a snack later on. My Danish parents Gunvar and Frederick thought I was selfish and I thought they were nosey. On one especially cold evening, after dinner, they confronted me about the candy bar and many other behaviors that they found strange in me. I had a real fear of being kicked out of my foster home in America because I didn't fit in there. I tried my best to avoid being close so that I wouldn't miss anyone when I was kicked out. Now these Danish parents had cornered me and one of my worse nightmares was coming true. I was about to get kicked out of this new yet temporary home.

Growing up walking on eggshells had taught me many things that helped to prepare me for this moment. I didn't argue but agreed with them and then thanked them for pointing out my weaknesses and then I pleaded with them to help me learn how to fit into their family. I had learned how to fit into the family in America but these people spoke directly to each other, they bathed in a public bath together and talked to each other like siblings or friends. There were no obvious rules in this house so I had felt a sense of calm and maybe a pleasant feeling living there. We came to an agreement not to kick me out and they would give me one more chance to fit in. My next thought was, run!

I thought where could I sneak off to that is nice and warm and would give me some time to come up with a new plan for how to stay in their home, I was getting used to them. The Danish national travel agency liked for Danes to travel and made it very inexpensive. If you pack a small bag and camp out in their office downtown you can go almost anywhere for 50.00 with a Days Notice. It was a bargain even back then. Being so far away from my American family was wonderful, another chance to try out being someone new.

The travel agency was located in the busy shopping district in downtown Kobenhavn and there were venders selling fresh peas in carts along the walking street outside. I stopped to buy a bag, as was the custom there to eat them raw right out of their pods. As I put another mouthful of bitter sweet peas in my mouth, I stepped through the doorway of the small office and looked across the room to see the most handsome young man, tall, tan, blue eyes and messy blonde hair, like the Danish version of one of the Beach Boys. His nametag read Soren. He looked up at me and smiled like a movie star and then called me over using an expression reserved for little girls. It was an expression my Scottish grandfather used with me only this time in Danish.

I felt this warm flush come over my face and I was 9 years old again smiling back at him as if some handsome uncle was about to greet me after a long separation. I told him that I was missing warm weather and beaches and he told me that he was taking a group of senior citizens to Africa that day and they had one seat left. Fifty dollars would cover airfare, hotel and one meal a day for a week if I wanted to go. So I rung up my Danish mother Gunvar and apologized for the short notice about the sun and the beaches in Africa and off I went. His smile could melt ice and he had this charming nervous giggle when he was speaking English. He laughed at my

## The Moving Pen

Danish and at my stories so that was all I needed to feel comfortable on my adventure. We boarded a direct flight to Africa and Soren asked me to sit next to him. As I chatted away, I thought of how my father said that I talked too much and should have my tongue bobbed because it must be too long for my mouth, thus the need to have it wagging all the time. I never knew if he would really do it or not so I didn't talk so much around my father.

I was expecting "Lions and tigers and bears oh my." Much to my surprise, as we flew in everything looked flat and rather barren. I didn't know exactly where we were going and had certainly never heard of Tunisia. It is the smallest country in Africa located along the Mediterranean Sea. Most of the buildings were white and had an Arabic feel to them. Although Arabic was the official language, about 80 percent of the population spoke French. There were lots of little houses and shacks along the beach side road the bus traveled along, then a beautiful white sandy stretch of beach and miles of ocean, just like my home on Nantucket.

Well no lions and jungle but at least I could lay out on the beach. Soren informed me that in coming at the last minute I would be the only one staying at a different hotel. He assured me it was nice and he would pick me up for tours if I wanted to join the others. When the bus pulled up to my hotel it looked more like one of those motels you see on the highway that should be abandoned but is still in use. I spoke French back then, which to my surprise was all that was spoken there. They thought that I was Danish and couldn't speak French so I had to put up with listening to the awful waiters comments about Danish girls. My room wasn't too bad; there were two twin beds, clean cement floors and an en suite bathroom. My room opened right out to the beach.

I spent the first few days laying out on the beach listening to French speaking gypsies walking their camels and soliciting people to take a ride. I had a lot of people trying to get me to go with them, which was flattering at first. It took me three days to notice that I was often the only woman on the beach each day and the only person in a bikini so maybe my popularity was not about me exactly.

The third day was eventful for two reasons, I woke up from my regular beach nap to something stepping on me, scratching and hissing. I was covered with iguanas, not little lizards but huge two-foot long snake faced dragons. They had five fingers with fat stubby nails on each limb and a spine that looked like a tree saw standing up on its edge. I couldn't scream I was frozen preparing to have a heart attack right there.

Out of the corner of my eye, I saw one of the motel waiters approaching me. As he came towards me he pulled a huge knife out of the case on his belt. He held it by the blade in one hand and raised his arm and then suddenly threw it right at me. It found its way right to a large iguana on my leg and the others scattered leaving me shivering like it was cold outside.

The waiter picked up his knife with the impaled iguana still on it and simply walked away. In addition I now had a roommate. I've forgotten her name but she was from Canada, and the motel director said they were full up, I had an extra bed and she spoke English so there you go. She was a much older woman at 24 and seemed so worldly. We spent the next morning talking on the beach about all her adventures backpacking around the world. Now there were two women on the beach and more gypsies were chatting us up. My roommate decided that one in particular was handsome so she got on his camel and rode off down the beach. I decided to look up Soren and the elderly Danish people. They were headed out for another bus tour of the countryside. Several Danish ladies reminded me that red heads burn easily. As often happens I had forgotten my fathers advice and got a good burn so the bus ride out of the sun seemed like a good idea, and Soren would be there.

The bus driver said, "A woman should fill a teacup with her tears for the shame of having a baby girl" as he stopped in front of a vast graveyard.

We saw so many small pink graves stones with various types of cups at their bases. The light blue graves were larger and neatly kept as it was a greater sin to have a son die. Soren spoke to us in Danish so as not to offend the bus driver. He said that the law about killing baby girls had changed recently but it was still the practice to kill or abandon any first-born children who weren't male.

I thought to myself how thankful I was to be abandoned in America where I'd had the chance to survive. I looked at all those pink graves and wondered about those little girls, my face felt flushed and my stomach churned so I quickly imagined them somewhere else growing up laughing and playing. Two veiled women outside looked up at the bus and nodded respectfully as they walked by, then turned in to the graveyard. We were all thankful to be visitors and not have to live in a place like this. Soren laughed at my short story about the iguanas and told me that my long red hair was beautiful. He said he could tell that I was a Danish/American because I looked Danish but talked so much I had to be American. I told him he was so smart that I couldn't fool him. I loved the complement and didn't want to tell him that I was a blank with an unknown background. Maybe I could learn how to be Danish and fit in my new family.

My views on lying were that it was fine to lie about myself but I was always honest about anything else. I had become an expert on lying about myself; it was a survival skill of sorts. Living was like sitting in a little boat adrift on the sea always weary of waves and wind that might rock it or tip it over. I tried very hard not to let anyone actually get in my boat or try to disturb it, it was safer that way. I thought that a little lie now and then was fine. My life was lots of lies made up by other people older than me so that just opened the door to my imagination. It was fun to make things up now and then when talking to strangers. I could pretend to be anyone when I was traveling, like taking a taxi to go try on expensive high heels and then putting your Keds back on to catch a bus.

When they dropped me off at my motel I waved good-bye and said I would see them all on the plane back to Denmark the next day. There were a lot of people in the motel living room attending a wedding. The bride was wearing a western style wedding dress and high top converse tennis shoes and tons of gold jewelry. The groom was barefoot and his pants were too short and he was the only one smiling, funny the things you remember. I remember how things looked, people's faces, and the colour of their clothing or hair but can't hold on to names and dates.

Dad says I can't find my way out of a paper bag with a flashlight and a map. Which has often been true but I had been doing well so far on this trip. I smiled at the bride and made my way back to my room. I opened the door to find two maids going through my bag. I asked what they were doing and without saying a word they ran out. A few minutes later the motel manager, the maids and 3 soldiers opened the door without knocking. They all started yelling in French.

"Where are the blankets, who do you work for and where is the money?"

I learned a lot about Tunisia and the culture in a very short time in that room. The wool blankets that were on the beds were gone and wool is a luxury there. Teenage girls such as me don't travel alone or wear pants unless they are hookers. They don't wear gold necklaces and watches and rings unless they have a lot of money. I assured them that I was a college student in Denmark and I did not have experience as a streetwalker. I told them to ask my roommate and was told that she went off with gypsies the day before and couldn't be found. If I didn't produce those blankets I was going to jail.

If you haven't been to jail before let me advise you that Tunisia is not the place to start. They tied my hands and whisked me right off to jail. Someone coined the term ignorance is bliss but my French was excellent back then and I heard and understood everything they said there, definitely no bliss. They had no intension of calling anyone and figured they would all take turns with me and then sell me. I had pretended not to understand up to that point and decided that I needed to use my acting skills as if there was an Emmy waiting for my performance. Late that night the first soldier came into my cell to grab me and I started to yell at him in French, "Ne me touchez pa."

I told him that my father was Italian mafia and that he and my husband would kill them all if they laid a hand on me. Growing up with a psychiatrist and friends whose parents are also psychiatrists had given me some field training in how to act a little crazy or a lot crazy. I stayed awake all that night defending myself and thought; "this is it I am going to be used and sold as a slave today." Around mid afternoon my luck changed, I looked up and saw Soren.

He started to yell at me in Danish, "Don't respond just listen to me. I told them that you are my wife and my property, that we had a fight and you ran off alone to that motel."

I thought my god, I've found a kindred spirit, and he is just as good a liar as I am.

Soren had boarded the plane and seeing that I wasn't there he got off and went to look for me. I got on my knees and shed some real tears for Soren and the soldiers. When they opened the door and let me out Soren grabbed me and gave me a big hug and a kiss. He was as tall as a lamppost and beautiful to look at. As he paid those awful people a large sum of money to get me back all I could think of was he was like the prince in my dreams who rushes in to save me as I am dying.

We caught a late flight out of Tunisia and I was unusually tired and quite, sleeping on Soren's shoulder most of the way back. As we stepped off the plane and descended the stairway, the cold wind slapped my sunburned face and sunk into my cheekbones making them ache. It was so early in the morning that it was still dark outside and the air had the smell of the ocean and fireplaces smoldering. Soren lived somewhere in Kobenhaven and I lived out along the coast. He asked me if I was all right and took me to catch the first train out of town to the little coastal village I lived in. I got on the train and waved good-bye and then sat down to rest a bit more on the long ride back to Runsted Kyst.

The sweater I had learned to knit with my Danish mother was scratching my sunburn so I pulled out a pen to write, "get lotion" on my hand. It's so hard to remember things like, "put lotion on before going out in the sun."

I walked along the cobblestone path to my home at No.3 Drosselvej a little weary of what the reception would be. Gunvar was at the door and pulled me in with a big smile on her face. The whole family had been waiting for me to get back and tried to prepare an American breakfast for me.

Gunvar and Frederick wanted to understand American children and had been thinking of how to make me more comfortable in their home. I told them I had a nice time but had gotten a sunburn. I spent the next year pretending to be the little sister in this Danish family and when I left I promised that I would be back.

I never managed to get back. I often think of them and Soren wondering why I didn't ask if I could see him again or why he never asked to see me. When I see fresh peas in the local market I buy a big bag and eat them right out of the pods before going home. With each bittersweet mouthful I close my eyes and think how happy I would be to repeat that whole trip just for the few hours where Soren pretended to be my husband and came back to save me. All my dreams came true for a few hours, Soren pretended to be my husband, I felt loved and safe and he laughed at my stories.

# Biographies

**Ursula Austin** came to Nantucket on her honeymoon wound up staying. She is co-author of a published book of poetry, *Healing*, and continues to write as well as study and teach Tai Chi, for which she has won three medals in competition.

**Kristine Glazer** has been a "summer" visitor to the island since 1991. In June 2012 she made Nantucket her home.

**Joanna Z. Greenfield** has worked with animals in Uganda and Israel. Her account of being attacked by a hyena was published in *The New Yorker* in 1996. Now living on Nantucket, she is facilitates projects designed to help communities with sustainable technologies.

**Amy Jenness** is a member of the Moors Poetry Collective and has poems published in three MPC anthologies. She is the programming coordinator for the Nantucket Atheneum and is currently working on a book for The History Press.

As a twelfth generation islander, **Julianne Kever** has Nantucket in her blood, breath and bones. Raised in a family of eleven children, she read as a way to retreat and books became her good friends. Julie writes poetry and is a founding member of the Moving Pen.

A native of Providence R.I. and frequent visitor to Nantucket, **Paula Korn** moved to the island in 2013. She has worked at Boeing Company and NASA, as well as in television. Retired from the corporate world, she is involved with projects relating to space exploration and her creative writing.

**Charles Manghis** grew up on Cape Cod and has raised three daughters on Nantucket. He has worked as an artist and carpenter on the island for many years.

# Biographies

**Harry Patz, Jr.** has visited Nantucket since 1995 and purchased a seasonal home here in 2011. His first novel, *The Naïve Guys: A Memoir of Friendship, Love and Tech in the Early 90s*, will be published in 2014. Harry is president of Gondolin Advisors LLC.

**Terry Norton's** grandfather purchased property and started coming to Nantucket in the early 1920s and her family has been coming ever since. Growing up, she always thought how amazing it would be to live on the island year round and made it a reality in 2006.

**Daryl Westbrook** has been on Nantucket for every summer of her life. She and her husband moved here permanently in 1996 and have a small real estate office in 'Sconset. She has a short story in the book of essays *The Little Gray Island*.

**The Moving Pen: Nantucket Atheneum Writer's Group** formed in May of 2013 and meets twice a month at the library to write together. The writing sessions are open to all and offered for free. *The Moving Pen* anthology is the first book published by the group. The Nantucket Atheneum is the island's public library.

Made in the USA
Charleston, SC
28 September 2014